THE *New* YANKEES
CENTURY

THE *New* YANKEES CENTURY

FOR THE
LOVE OF JETER,
JOLTIN' JOE, AND
MARIANO

ALAN ROSS

Cumberland House
Nashville, Tennessee

THE NEW YANKEES CENTURY
PUBLISHED BY CUMBERLAND HOUSE PUBLISHING, INC.
431 Harding Industrial Drive
Nashville, TN 37211-3160

Cover design: Gore Studio, Inc.
Text design: John Mitchell

Library of Congress Cataloging-in-Publication Data

The New Yankees century : for the love of Jeter, Joltin' Joe, and
Mariano / [edited by] Alan Ross.
    p. cm.
  Includes bibliographical references (p. 247) and index.
  ISBN-13: 978-1-58182-526-8 (pbk. : alk. paper)
  ISBN-10: 1-58182-526-9 (pbk. : alk. paper)
  1. New York Yankees (Baseball team)—History—Quotations,
maxims, etc. I. Ross, Alan, 1944–
  GV875.N4N48 2006
  796.357'64097471—dc22
  ISBN: 978-1-68442-159-6   2006003858

Derek Jeter

NEW YORK YANKEES

CONTENTS

	Introduction	*9*
	Remembrance	*11*
1	Yankee Tradition	13
2	Pinstripe Pride	21
3	Yankees in Pinstripes	27
4	Pinstripe Character	43
5	Stengelese and Yogi-isms	53
6	Pinstripe Legends	65
7	Shrine to No. 7	105
8	Pinstripe Humor	115
9	Great Moments	123
10	The Great Yankee Teams	145
11	New York Yankees All-Time Team	157
12	Fields of Play	169
13	THE Rivalry	179
14	The Subway Series	187
15	Life	197
16	The Bronx Clubhouse	205
17	World Champion Rosters	219
	Bibliography	*247*
	Index	*251*

INTRODUCTION

A friend once asked me if I had ever seen the great Joe DiMaggio.

"Does an Old-Timers game count?"

He assured me that it did.

In that case, I consider myself fortunate to have seen the legendary Yankee Clipper in action. It was approximately 12 to 13 seasons after his retirement in 1951, and although his head was significantly graying, Joltin' Joe stroked a double on a rope to left-center that clearly gave a hint to the power that once lurked there in his prime.

The New Yankees Century is DiMag and Yogi, Casey and The Mick, Reggie and Thurman, Mariano and Derek, and the overwhelming galaxy of timeless stars that ultimately brought the second Yankees century into being. It is a compendium of the men in pinstripes told primarily through the voices of the players, coaches, managers, opponents, and sportswriters—a living retrospective on sport's greatest ongoing phenomenon: the Bronx Bombers.

In this new edition, two chapters and more than 65 pages have been added to the original text. Extra photos adorn the pages.

If recollection of the numberless heroes in Yankee navy blue and white stirs the innards of your soul, read on.

It's quintessential pinstripe.

REMEMBRANCE

It was a Saturday afternoon, Sept. 20, 1952, when I first met Yankee Stadium. The *old* Yankee Stadium. The one with the turquoise-colored art-deco copper-frieze facade that rimmed the roofline from the grandstand in left field all the way around to right— a sublime vision worthy of gawking.

Yes, I too had the Billy Crystal my-father-took-me-to-my-first-big-league-ball-game-at-Yankee-Stadium-I-was-shocked-by-how-green-the-grass-was experience when I was seven.

It's amazing what you remember: My parents and I sat in a box just to the left of home plate (I thought at the time they were lousy seats because you had to look through the wire screen to see the action). I can still see Hank Bauer, the Yankees' right fielder, racing around third in bright sunlight and barreling home into the long shadows that reached out from behind home plate to the infield grass, scoring from first on an eighth-inning double by Yogi Berra.

The opponent that day was the Philadelphia Athletics—they of Connie Mack lore and the future Kansas City-Oakland A's. I still vividly recall

Athletics first baseman Ferris Fain popping up to the infield and throwing his bat in disgust, end over end, high into the sky. I gaped. It looked like the bat went higher than the ball. One more item of note: The Yanks, of course, behind Eddie Lopat's four-hitter, posted a 2–0 win.

There would be other trips to the hallowed Mecca of Bronx Bomberdom. Other days when a Moose Skowron home run barely curled around the right-field flagpole in the lower stands. Other times to be thrilled by an opposite-field golfed homer by The Mick. And there was that rare double-header win by pitcher Johnny Kucks.

It all translates to the heartthrob of youth—me and my Yankees.

I was lucky. I didn't just get to hear or read about my heroes—Berra, Ford, Mantle, Bauer, Martin, Rizzuto, Reynolds, Lopat, Raschi. I actually got to see them: Mantle, head bowed, trotting in from center field. Swarthy Yogi taking off his catcher's mask. Both of them returning to the dugout after an inning's work in the field. Those moments go beyond treasure, and I feel the circle turning as others before me doubtless felt upon viewing Ruth, Gehrig, Meusel, Gómez, Dickey, DiMaggio, Henrich. Haunting apparitions to later generations of fans, but larger than life for those who witnessed them on the field.

And through it all there has been one constant— the magnificent stadium. The grand overseer. The guardian of the magic. The keeper of the pinstripes.

—A.R.

1

YANKEE TRADITION

The players, the stadium, the pinstripes, "five o'clock lightning," the innumerable Yankee come-from-behind wins, the legend that transcends myth. Blend it all together and you have a 26-time world champion. That's more than one-quarter of the 96 championships played in the previous century.

Some teams—Brooklyn/Los Angeles, Oakland, and Cincinnati come to mind—are fortunate to have had one dynasty in their franchise's history. Some teams never even field one. The Yankees have had five. Five separate dynasties.

No greater tradition ever existed.

The myth of the Yankee pinstripe, which insisted that merely putting on the Yankee uniform made you part of a remorseless, invincible team, did not yet exist. The 1927 club carved out its beginnings.

John Mosedale
writer/author

It's always questionable whether we have the best talent, player for player, from season to season. Who can say that? But as a club, we've been able to incorporate all the aspects of our game and put it together for a team effort....Anyone on our team can beat you.

Bernie Williams
center field (1991–)

The essence of the Yankees is that they win. From in front or from behind, they win. And that's why the history of the New York Yankees is virtually the history of baseball.

Dave Anderson
New York Times

When we were challenged, when we had to win, we stuck together and played with a fury and determination that could only come from team spirit. We had a pride in our performance that was very real. It took on the form of snobbery. We felt we were superior people, and I do believe we left a heritage that became a Yankee tradition.

Waite Hoyt
pitcher (1921–30)

Just putting on a Yankee uniform gave me a little confidence, I think. That club could carry you. You were better than you actually were.

Mark Koenig
shortstop (1925–30)

To be a Yankee is a thought in everyone's head. . . . Just walking into Yankee Stadium, chills run through you. I believe there was a higher offer, but no matter how much money is offered, if you want to be a Yankee, you don't think about it.

Jim "Catfish" Hunter
*pitcher (1975–79),
on his heralded free-agency
signing, New Year's Eve 1974*

Five o'clock lightning," once phrased by Earle Combs and referring to the team's ability to strike so often in the late innings, caught on, spread through the league and seeped into the consciousness of opposing pitchers. They began to dread the approach of five o'clock and the eighth inning.

Frank Graham
legendary sportswriter

When you go to other parks, they hang banners for the wild-card or Eastern Division or Western Division champions. Around here, they don't hang anything unless it's for being world champions.

Chili Davis
outfield/designated hitter
(1998–99)

Even though I have loyalty to people, you have to be loyal to 25 players as opposed to just one.

Joe Torre
manager (1996–)

When the Yankees came to town, it was like Barnum and Bailey coming to town . . . it was the excitement. They had these gray uniforms, but there was a blue hue to them. I'll never forget them. Watching them warm up was as exciting as watching the game. Being in Cleveland, you couldn't root for them, but you could boo them in awe.

George Steinbrenner
Yankees owner (1973–),
on growing up in Cleveland

The Yankees will never be beaten. They will only wear out.

New York Sun
1927

When I came here, I was told there's two seasons: regular season and postseason. There's not too many teams I've played for who expect to get to the postseason. This team has been there enough that they expect to get to the postseason every year.

Randy Johnson
pitcher (2005–)

During the 1920s, New York Yankee owner Jacob Ruppert once described his perfect afternoon at Yankee Stadium. "It's when the Yankees score eight runs in the first inning," Ruppert said, "and then slowly pull away."

Peter Golenbock
author,
Dynasty: The New York Yankees
(1975)

You kind of took it for granted around the Yankees that there was always going to be baseball in October.

Whitey Ford
pitcher (1950, 1953–67)

No other team in baseball can match their tradition, but no team is better at living up to their tradition than the Yankees.

Glenn Stout
author

2

PINSTRIPE PRIDE

*E*very moviegoer of the last half-century has seen Gary Cooper's stirring portrayal of the immortal Lou Gehrig in Pride of the Yankees.

But the great Iron Horse wasn't the only wearer of the pinstripes to don an attitude of unbeatable pride during his Yankee days. Such first-magnitude stars as Jim "Catfish" Hunter, Reggie Jackson, Roger Clemens, and Johnny Damon all could have opted for bigger paychecks somewhere else but ultimately chose to pull on the pinstripes. A player who has achieved the stature of Clemens, with seven Cy Young Awards, desires to experience the absolute ultimate sometime during his career.

Deep down they all intuit the empirical truth: Nothing beats being a Yankee.

I think of myself as a Yankee.

Mark Koenig

who, during his 12-year major-league career, also played with the Detroit Tigers, Chicago Cubs, Cincinnati Reds, and New York Giants

---

Billy Crystal did a sketch for *Saturday Night Live*, talking about how his dad took him to a game one time, and then he says, "Mick hit one out of the park. It was a good day." That's nice, really nice, to have people feel that way.

Mickey Mantle

center field (1951–68), 1994

I don't think [Casey Stengel] ever cared about your color if you wore the Yankee uniform with pride.

Elston Howard

catcher-outfield (1955–67), nine-time AL All-Star, 1963 AL MVP

Even now I look up to him, he's never disappointed me.

Andy Pafko
*17-year National League player
and four-time All-Star,
on Joe DiMaggio*

————

I'm proud to introduce the man who succeeded me in centerfield in 1951.

Joe DiMaggio
*center field (1936–42; 1946–51),
introducing Mickey Mantle to
the sold-out crowd at Yankee
Stadium on Mickey Mantle Day,
September 1965*

————

Lou Gehrig was the most valuable player the Yankees ever had because he was a prime source of their greatest asset: an implied confidence in themselves and in every man on the club. Lou's pride as a big leaguer rubbed off on every one who played with him.

Stanley Frank
sportswriter

For 16 years into every ball park in which I have ever walked, I received nothing but kindness and encouragement. Mine has been a full life. . . . I have been privileged to play many years with the famous Yankees, the greatest team of all times. . . . I may have been given a bad break, but I have an awful lot to live for. All in all, I can say on this day that I consider myself the luckiest man on the face of the earth.

Lou Gehrig
*first base (1923–39),
from his farewell speech on
Lou Gehrig Appreciation Day,
July 4, 1939*

I never knew how someone who was dying could say he was the luckiest man in the world. But now I understand.

Mickey Mantle

June 8, 1969, referring to Lou Gehrig's immortal farewell speech the day Mantle's No. 7 was retired at Yankee Stadium

The ghosts of Ruth and Gehrig, DiMaggio and Mantle seem to hover over the stadium, inspiring the current wearers of the sacred pinstripes with a confidence no other team can match—Yankee pride—and perhaps from time to time nudging a ball over the fence or into a glove—Yankee luck.

Kenneth Auchincloss

writer, Newsweek, *Oct. 30, 2000*

If you're a Yankee fan, or if you're not a Yankee fan—you have to admit, we're winners.

Paul O'Neill
*outfield (1993–2001),
after the 2000 World Series*

We are the New York Yankees.

George Steinbrenner

3

YANKEES IN PINSTRIPES

*E*very follower of the Bronx Bombers can call the roll of imposing Yankee superstars—Ruth, Gehrig, Dickey, DiMaggio, Mantle, Maris, Berra, Ford, Munson, Guidry, Jackson, Hunter, Nettles, Mattingly, Jeter, Rivera, Rodriguez . . .

But a galaxy of others have contributed to the great Yankee mosaic: Charley "King Kong" Keller, Spud Chandler, Joe Gordon, Tommy Henrich, Vic Raschi, Allie Reynolds, Bobby Murcer, Bobby Richardson, Tony Kubek, Joe Pepitone, Sparky Lyle, Paul O'Neill, Tino Martinez, Bernie Williams.

And then there are those unsung gladiators who daily toiled in relative obscurity: the Koenigs, Careys, Cervs, Clarks, Sojos, and many more.

All have worn the vaunted pinstripes; all will forever share a place in Yankee lore.

If you were to cut that bird's head open, the weakness of every batter in the league would fall out.

Anonymous Yankee coach
on Hall of Fame pitcher
Herb Pennock (1923–33)

You didn't face a left-hander, you faced Herb Pennock.

Harry Heilmann
Hall of Famer and four-time AL
batting champion with Detroit,
to teammate Bob "Fatty"
Fothergill, who boasted that no
left-hander could get him out
(Fothergill went 0–for–4 against
Pennock)

Tony Lazzeri was "Poosh 'Em Up," a name dating back to his first year in organized baseball, with Salt Lake City, when he was struggling, and a restaurant owner named Tony Roffetti took pity on him, feeding him spaghetti dinners three nights' running, and urging him to "poosh 'em up," meaning hit.

John Mosedale

He didn't discover America, but then Columbus never went behind third for an overthrow to cut off the tying run in the ninth inning.

New York Times
on Tony Lazzeri

Bob Meusel

NEW YORK YANKEES

Left-fielder Bob Meusel had, by common consent, the best arm in baseball—a rifle, who also hit for the average (.315 in 1926) and with power. The only year during the 1920s that Ruth did not lead the league in home runs—1925—Meusel was the leader, with 33, and the runs-batted-in leader too.

John Mosedale

He had lightnin' on the ball.

Casey Stengel
*manager (1949–60),
on Meusel*

There was never any more doubt about Earle Combs' athletic prowess than about his character. Of the latter, Joe McCarthy said, "Earle Combs is the greatest gentleman in baseball"; as to the other, Gehrig moved Joe DiMaggio over to make room in center field for Combs on his all-time Yankee team.

John Mosedale

It's all over boys. Here comes Frank Merriwell.

Dan Howley
St. Louis Browns manager, on Yankees reliever Wilcy Moore, a 30-year-old rookie phenom in 1927, who won 19 games for New York, recording a league-high 13 saves

He has rather a spare and meager frame, when he stands with his bat poised expectantly and his thin legs somewhat apart, his body forward, he suggests a kangaroo ready for take-off. His antics in the field are also in character. The way he darts about, scooping up grounders with the full play of those long arms and legs of his reminds you of a toy jumping jack on a string.

***Baseball* magazine**
on third baseman "Jumping Joe" Dugan

Fellows like Ruth and Gehrig can ruin an ordinary ballplayer. They win so many games by their individual efforts that you wonder why you are in the lineup.

Joe Dugan
third base (1922–28)

That guy can hit me in the middle of the night, blindfolded and with two broken feet to boot.

Bob Feller
*Cleveland Indians Hall of Fame pitcher (1936–56),
on Tommy Henrich*

Hank Bauer had a face that was once described as "looking like a clenched fist."

Maury Allen
author/sportswriter for the
New York Post

The Chief's glare scared me, and we were on the same team!

Whitey Ford
*on Allie "the Chief" Reynolds,
a Yankee mainstay, along with
Vic Raschi, from the late 1940s
through mid-'50s. Reynolds threw
two no-hitters during the 1951
season and posted 131 wins
during eight seasons in New York*

I always felt the pitcher had the advantage, like serving in tennis.

Allie Reynolds
pitcher (1947–54)

My best pitch is anything the batter grounds, lines, or pops in the direction of Phil Rizzuto.

Vic Raschi
pitcher (1946–53)

That little punk—how I love 'im!

Casey Stengel
on Billy Martin

Ralph Houk is the best manager I ever played for.

Mickey Mantle

It took me a while to get smart. There are certainly many things a ballplayer can do offensively besides hitting homers.

Bobby Murcer
outfield (1965–66, 1969–74, 1979–83)

Clete Boyer was the best third baseman I've ever seen, bar none. Brooks Robinson was great. Graig Nettles was great. But Clete was a better defensive player. No one could dive to the right, backhand the ball, and throw from his knees like Clete.

Tony Kubek
shortstop (1957–65)

Tino Martinez is definitely the heart and soul of this team. He's actually a lot like Don Mattingly—same intensity, ready to play every day. He has a lot of Mattingly's leadership qualities.

David Cone
pitcher (1995–2000)

George Steinbrenner described him as a warrior, and I think that is a perfect fit for him. . . . Paul O'Neill is the backbone of this ball club.

Joe Torre

I approach every at-bat the same, you continue to battle. The big thing with two strikes is not to panic. The key for me is to try to stick with what I do and not try to get into the pitcher's head.

Paul O'Neill

I never take this job for granted. I never lose sight of the ones who have come before me out there. It's not just Mr. DiMaggio and Mickey Mantle. You think about Bobby Murcer and Mickey Rivers. You think about the kind of center field Paul Blair played when he was a Yankee. The truth is, the best thing for me is to not think about those people too much. The best thing for me is to keep going.

Bernie Williams

FAST FACT: In 1998 Williams became the first player to win a batting title, Gold Glove Award, and a World Series championship in the same season. Sharing honors with switch-hitting teammate Jorge Posada, Williams was part of the only pair of teammates to hit homers from both sides of the plate in the same game.

Andy Pettitte's a great pitcher. He throws that cutter and there's little you can do.

Bubba Trammell
New York Mets outfielder
(2000, 2003)

He's good. He's got a good arm, and he's got that funky fastball.

John Gibbons
Toronto manager,
on rookie pitcher Chien-Ming
Wang, who went 8–5 in 2005

He's so good in his preparation. He's so darned determined.

Joe Torre
on Hideki Matsui

If the Yankees had 25 Matsuis, they would have won the 2003 World Series

Joel Sherman
New York Post *baseball*
columnist

It's taken him a long time. And guys who stay with it to this point, the determination is there, the know-how, the intelligence on how to pitch.

Joe Torre

on 33-year-old first-year-Yankee pitching sensation Aaron Small, called up from AAA Columbus because of the attrition on the Yankees' staff in midsummer 2005. Small showed poise and maturity in compiling an impressive 10–0 record with New York

It hurts to think about where we would be without these guys. They've been a godsend.

Alex Rodriguez

third base (2004–), on the surprise pitching contributions from first-year Yankees Aaron Small (10–0) and Shawn Chacon (7–3), both of whom joined New York in mid-2005 with the Yanks' rotation beset by injuries

The thing about Sheff is, even if he's not 100 percent he's still intimidating. You just feel he's going to find a way to get it done.

Joe Torre
on right-fielder Gary Sheffield

I put him up there with Mariano Rivera as one of the greatest competitors that I've ever played against. It's kind of weird seeing him in a different uniform.

Alex Rodriguez
on former teammate Orlando "El Duque" Hernández, who pitched for the White Sox in 2005 before being traded to Arizona in the 2005–06 off-season

He has no fear.

Joe Torre
on Gary Sheffield

That's the exciting part about being a Yankee. Whenever you do anything special, you're joining Ruth, Gehrig, Mantle, DiMaggio.

Jason Giambi

first base (2002–),
after hitting his 299th and
300th career homers against the
Los Angeles Angels of Anaheim,
July 31, 2005

My job is to go up and set up in the eighth inning to get to Rivera in the ninth. That's what my job is going to be for the next three years. Whatever happens after that will happen.

Kyle Farnsworth

pitcher (2006–),
obtained from Atlanta after the
2005 season and heir apparent
to Rivera as Yankee closer

He should be here a long time.

Josh Towers

Toronto Blue Jays pitcher,
on 2005 rookie second base
sensation Robinson Cano

4

PINSTRIPE CHARACTER

Gehrig set his record of 2,130 consecutive games in conditions he never bothered to complain about. Late in his career, x-rays of his hands revealed 17 fractures he had let heal by themselves. He had broken every finger in both hands, some twice, and didn't mention it. Hit by a pitch that gave him a concussion that should have put him in bed for a week, he came to the park the following day and got four hits.

John Mosedale

You play the game to win the game, and not worry about what's on the back of the baseball card at the end of the year.

Paul O'Neill

⊷⧆⊶

Mantle is the only man I ever saw who was crippled who could outdo the world.

Casey Stengel

⊷⧆⊶

I watched him bandage that knee—the whole leg—and I saw what he had to go through every day to play. He was taped from shin to thigh. And now I'll never be able to say enough in praise. Seeing those legs, his power becomes unbelievable.

Early Wynn

23-year major-league pitcher and Hall of Famer,
on Mickey Mantle, at an All-Star game in the late 1950s

There could be a kid who may be seeing me for the first or last time. I owe him my best.

Joe DiMaggio
asked why he always played hard, even when a game was hopelessly lost or already won

---

I ask only one thing of my players—hustle. It doesn't take any ability to hustle.

Billy Martin
second base (1950–53, 1955–57)/manager (1975–78, 1979, 1983, 1985, 1988)

If you bawl your players out while they're losing, they may punch you in the nose. Do it while they're winning and they'll listen.

Casey Stengel
on player handling, learned as a player under New York Giants manager John McGraw

You can't say anything too good about Roger Maris. He ran right through a wooden fence for me at Keokuk. I thought he was out for the year, but he held the ball, came to, and got up and won the game for me with a homer in the ninth. How much hustle can a guy give you?

Jo-Jo White

Maris's manager in the Class B Three-I League in Keokuk, Iowa

⸺⁑⸺

When you have to go through tough times, I think winning is more satisfying.

Joe Torre

⸺⁑⸺

He made me feel part of the club. He made me feel I was a Yankee.

Elston Howard

catcher/left field (1955–67) and the Yankees' first African-American player, on Casey Stengel

I have always been a great admirer of Casey Stengel. He was a great manager and showed great strength of character. I don't think anybody contributed more to baseball than Casey Stengel. He ranks right up there with Ty Cobb, Babe Ruth, and Judge Landis.

Ted Williams
Boston Red Sox legend

It's something inside his heart that's bigger than anything. He's got the heart of a lion about to grab something.

Darryl Strawberry
outfield/designated hitter
(1995–99),
on David Cone

When he goes out there, he spills his guts out.

Mel Stottlemyre
pitcher (1964–74)/coach
(1996–2005),
on David Cone

They just keep coming at you. It reminds me of great fighters—heavyweights who just won't let up. They come at you and wear you down. You think, "I'm gonna get 'em," but you don't.

George Steinbrenner
on his 2000 world champions

When you go through things with the same core of people, you never lose faith in them. And Joe [Torre] doesn't forget. That's a credit to him and what he's brought to this team.

Paul O'Neill

In Cuba, there is no relief pitching. . . . It's win or die.

Orlando "El Duque" Hernández
pitcher (1998–2004)

Even though a bunch of people had me retiring, I trust my stuff and I know who I am.

Mariano Rivera

pitcher (1995–),
after losing his first two save
opportunities—both to the
Boston Red Sox—to start the
2005 campaign. Rivera then
came back to record his career-
best 30th-consecutive save in
a row on Aug. 8, in a 3–2 victory
over the White Sox

The bottom line is it's never over until the last out. If you've done something before, you always think you can do it again.

Derek Jeter

shortstop (1996–)

Jorge Posada has tried to inspire the Yankees for the stretch run, handing out T-shirts to teammates that say "Grind It" on the front and "There is no trying, there is only doing or not doing" on the back.

Associated Press

before a 7–6 victory over Baltimore on Sept. 22, 2005, to move a game and a half ahead of Boston in the AL East. Posada backed up his T-shirt claim, hitting two home runs— his 11th career multi-homer game

I always feel like I can play through anything.

Gary Sheffield

right field (2004–), plagued by injuries through much of his Yankee tenure

I get nervous, I'm human. When I get out on the mound, that's where I'm supposed to be. I'm in control and nobody can bother me.

Shawn Chacon
pitcher (2005–)

We don't play to just make it to the play-offs; we've been to the playoffs before. We play to win.

Derek Jeter

It's very hard to always expect to do the things we're supposed to do as a team. But nonetheless, I think we as a team have the highest expectations.

Bernie Williams

Not relying on any one guy but getting contributions from every single person on this roster, that's how we win.

Derek Jeter

Pressure situations are really what the game is all about. It gives you so much joy to produce in situations when the game is on the line. You've got to make yourself think that's the situation you want to be in.

Bernie Williams
after hitting his 11th career grand slam to help the Yankees to their ninth straight win, a 6–3 victory over Seattle in mid-May 2005, the Bronx Bombers' longest winning streak in nearly four years.

When a team gives us an extra out, we jump on them. It's like chum in the water and our guys can smell it. Then they get after it. We go into our attack mode.

Roger Clemens
pitcher (1999–2003)

5

STENGELESE AND YOGI-ISMS

Baseball has birthed a wondrous gallery of odd-balls, cut-up comics, and colorful characters.

Two of the sport's most unique novelties wound up on the same team at the same time, a period of 12 years—the talented and entertaining Lawrence Peter Berra and Charles Dillon Stengel. Yogi and Casey to everyone.

The gems that emanated from these two magnificent assassins of the English language have had scribes scurrying to document their every dizzying word—and even some they didn't say.

Here is a smattering of some of the delightful chin music uttered from and about baseball's two most eloquent palaverists.

Yogi [Berra] is dumb like a fox. Not only on the ball field but off the field too.

Mickey Mantle

The 75 World Series games and the other records are not what make Yogi different. Yogi is what makes Yogi different. We had breakfast one time, and he looked at the menu and said, "I only have eggs in Cincinnati." I didn't ask him why, but you can bet he had a good reason.

Joe DiMaggio

It ain't over till it's over.

Yogi Berra
catcher (1946–63)

You can observe a lot by watching.

Yogi Berra

He's got birds in his garret.

Wilbert Robinson

former manager,
Brooklyn Dodgers,
on the classic Stengel bird bit,
June 6, 1918

FAST FACT: While with Pittsburgh, a teammate of Stengel's, Leon Cadore, saw a bird hit a brick wall in the Pirates' bullpen during pregame warmups at Ebbets Field. Cadore picked up the stunned bird and placed it under Stengel's cap. Stengel left it there. As the lead-off batter in the second inning, Stengel, an ex-Dodger player, was booed lustily by Dodger fans as he stepped up to the plate. In a gesture that has become legend, Stengel grandly doffed his cap to the crowd, which gasped as the bird took flight.

It gets late early out there.

Yogi Berra

*on Yankee Stadium's left field,
the sun field*

FAST FACT: Late afternoon shadows and the low-setting sun just above the facade behind first base create trying conditions for left fielders.

If you come to a fork in the road, take it.

Yogi Berra

Why buy good luggage? You only use it when you travel.

Yogi Berra

The future ain't what it used to be.

Yogi Berra

A nickel ain't worth a dime anymore.

Yogi Berra

I never coulda done it without my players.

Casey Stengel
after winning the 1949 American League pennant in his debut season as Yanks manager

———⚬———

I remember Casey way back. As early as 1925, he was talking Stengelese. It helped sell tickets.

Ken Smith
former newspaperman and director of baseball's Hall of Fame

———⚬———

Brooklyn was the borough of churches and bad ball clubs, many of which I had.

Casey Stengel
on his stint as Brooklyn Dodgers manager (1934–36)

———⚬———

Whenever I decided to release a guy, I always had his room searched first for a gun. You couldn't take any chances with those birds.

Casey Stengel

We had this left-hander, Gazzara [Bob Kuzava] and they had that brilliant Mr. Rob-A-Son at the plate and all of a sudden, whoops, here comes a slow ball when you expect a fastball, and why wouldn't you tap it into right field if you wuz right-handed, but Mr. Rob-A-Son tried to hit the ball over the building and instead he hit a ball up the shoot . . . and Mr. Collins, which was my first baseman, was counting his money so he never seen it, and Mr. Berra, my catcher, is standing with his hands on his hips yelling for Mr. Collins, and Mr. Gazzara did the pitching and he ain't about to do the catchin', so that leaves the second baseman, and you know who that is, to come in, lose his cap, and get it before it hits the grass, which if he did would be kicked because he was runnin' so fast and almost tripped over the mound which was a mountain in Brooklyn to help them sinkerball pitchers, Mr. [Carl] Erskine and them, and McGraw used to do that too, and why wouldn't ya, if you had spitters on the staff, but my rooster caught it and it didn't hit off his schnozz like a lot of them would have.

Casey Stengel

on Billy Martin's two-out seventh-inning infield catch against the Brooklyn Dodgers to save a 4–2 Yankees win in Game Seven of the 1952 World Series

It's déjà vu all over again.
Yogi Berra

I ain't in no slump . . . I just ain't hitting.
Yogi Berra

Bill Dickey is learning me his experience.
Yogi Berra
as a rookie in 1946

Ninety percent of the game is half mental.
Yogi Berra

Never answer an anonymous letter.
Yogi Berra

I didn't really say everything I said.
Yogi Berra

I had many years that I was not success-ful as a ballplayer, as it is a game of skill. And then I was no doubt discharged by baseball in which I had to go back to the minor leagues as a manager, and after being in the minor leagues as a manager, I became a major-league manager in sev-eral cities and was discharged; we call it discharged because there is no question I had to leave.

Casey Stengel
at the 1958 Senate subcommittee hearings investigating baseball's reserve clause

Just because your legs is dead doesn't mean your head is too.

Casey Stengel
at 71

Ruth, Gehrig, Huggins, someone throw that damn ball in here, now!

Casey Stengel

after a ball hit to deep center field in old Yankee Stadium rattled around the in-the-field-of-play stone monuments of Ruth, Gehrig, and Huggins

---

I know'd you'd wanna check that, so I looked it up. Why wouldn't ya use all the ones you got if ya needed hitting especially since my own fellas which is new and how do you know what they can do if they hadn't played a game for ya since it don't count yet and they don't get paid?

Casey Stengel

asked to evaluate his Yankee pitching staff in the spring of 1950

They examined all my organs. Some of them are quite remarkable and others are not so good. A lot of museums are bidding for them.

Casey Stengel

upon his release from Lenox Hill Hospital after a virus and high fever in May 1960

I commenced winning pennants when I came here, but I didn't commence getting any younger. . . . I'll never make the mistake of being 70 again.

Casey Stengel

at his Yankees resignation/ discharge press conference, Oct. 18, 1960

Some people my age are dead at the present time.

Casey Stengel

⸺⚬⸺

Can't anybody play this game!

Casey Stengel

6

PINSTRIPE LEGENDS

Some 20 years ago, I stopped talking about the Babe for the simple reason that I realized that those who had never seen him didn't believe me.

Tommy Holmes

11-year National League outfielder (1942–52)

To understand him, you had to understand this: He wasn't human. No human could have done the things he did and lived the way he lived and been a ballplayer. Cobb? Could he pitch? Speaker? The rest? I saw them. I was there. There was never anybody close. When you figure the things he did and the way he lived and the way he played, you got to figure he was more than animal even. There was never anyone like him. He was a god.

Joe Dugan
on Babe Ruth

It was figured that Ruth would hit home runs, but when he shocked baseball by hitting 59 in 1921, it was believed that the mark would last, in baseball time, forever.

John Mosedale

Ruth was a liberator who endeavored by personal example to show that no fun ever hurt you and that a bold spirit walks through the gloom ignoring old signposts, following instead his nose, a man uncorrupted by good living.

Heywood Broun
writer

Wasn't the Babe Sir Lancelot riding down Broadway wearing a camel's hair coat with a big cigar stuck in his mouth? Didn't he pick baseball up by the boot straps when it was rocked to the very foundation by the Black Sox Scandal? . . . People used to say they'd rather see him strike out with that tremendous flourish of his than see others knock the ball out of the park.

George Girsch
New York Daily Mirror

Babe Ruth had been a great pitcher, capable of making the Hall of Fame through that arduous calling alone, having once, as every schoolboy learns along with the pledge of allegiance, pitched 29⅔ scoreless World Series innings, a record that stood for 43 years. He had become an outfielder only because his bat was too explosive to leave out of the daily lineup, but he retained his marvelous arm, so that he never made a mechanical error, never threw to the wrong base.

John Mosedale

NEW YORK YANKEES

Babe Ruth

Sportswriters vied with one another to invent new nicknames for the Babe. One of the first had Italian origins—"The Bambino." It fit. Others were the "Behemoth of Bust," the "Rajah of Rap," the "Caliph of Clout," the "Maharajah of Mash," the "Wazir of Wham," and, of course, the "Sultan of Swat." His teammates simply called him "Jidge" or "Jidgie"—short for "George"—and he called most of them "Keed," since he could never remember their names.

Jay David
author

The fans applauded Ruth's home run. That's his business. Not so Gehrig's. He's just a first baseman.

New York Herald Tribune
April 1927, Philadelphia Athletics' home opener

FAST FACT: Ruth had hit his second home run of the year, in which he would ultimately hit 60; Gehrig hit his third, a blow "that landed on the roof of a home on 20th Street and bounced on and on." It was a harbinger of things to come for the Yankee Iron Horse. Gehrig's superlative career would never escape Ruth's gargantuan shadow.

He could be counted upon. He was there every day at the ballpark bending his back and ready to break his neck to win for his side. He was there day after day and year after year. He never sulked or whined or went into a pot or a huff. He was the answer to a manager's dream.

John Kieran
New York Times *sportswriter, on Lou Gehrig*

New York Yankees

Lou Gehrig

Lou Gehrig . . . he was the guy who hit all those homers the year Ruth set the record.

Franklin P. Adams
author/poet

I'm not a headline guy, and we might as well face it. I'm just a guy who's in the there every day. The fellow who follows the Babe in the batting order. When Babe's turn at bat is over, whether he strikes out or belts a home run, the fans are still talking about him when I come up. If I stood on my head at the plate, nobody'd pay any attention.

Lou Gehrig

He made you feel like a giant.

Mark Koenig
on manager Miller Huggins

Was Bill Dickey the greatest catcher the game has ever known? Connie Mack thought so, as did Ed Barrow and Ty Cobb.

**William Hageman
Warren Wilbert**
authors

He was a precisely controlled dynamo of fury: bat cocked high, feet planted wide, perfectly still until the final moment, when he advanced his left foot a mere inch or two and turned loose one of baseball's thunderbolt swings.

Donald Honig
*historian/author,
on Joe DiMaggio*

He is splendid in his line of work and we need him in there.

Casey Stengel
on Joe DiMaggio

Now wait a minute, you're going into too big a man. Maybe he woulda been an astronaut if he wanted. He could hit some balls off the moon and see if they'd carry. There were a lot of great ones and Ruth could pitch, too, but this fella is the best I ever had.

Casey Stengel
on Joe DiMaggio

When Joe came into the clubhouse it was like a senator or a president coming in.

Billy Martin
as a Yankee rookie in 1950, on the regal presence of teammate Joe DiMaggio

When he walked into the clubhouse, the lights flickered. Joe DiMaggio was a star.

Pete Sheehy
longtime Yankees clubhouse custodian

Joe DiMaggio

The best base runner I ever saw.

Joe McCarthy
manager (1931–46),
on Joe DiMaggio

———

There's so much ground out there in Yankee Stadium, the toughest center field in baseball. Only the great ones can play it. And he did it so easily. You never saw him make a great catch. You never saw him dive for a ball. He didn't have to. He was already there to catch it.

Joe McCarthy
on Joltin' Joe

———

I would like to take the great DiMaggio fishing. They say his father was a fisherman.

Ernest Hemingway
The Old Man and the Sea

You couldn't chip that bat. That's the way DiMaggio's wood was on the bats. He would ask for that type of wood. Being an old fisherman, he knew about the trees.

Phil Rizzuto
*shortstop (1941–42, 1946–56),
in* O Holy Cow!

Ty Cobb once said that only two players, Phil Rizzuto and Stan Musial, would have been stars in Cobb's time. He included Rizzuto's exceptional ability to hit to any field and to lay down a bunt where it was most effective, plus his all-around defensive genius.

Jay David

He is the greatest shortstop I have ever seen, and I have watched some beauties. Honus Wagner was a better hitter, but I've seen this kid make plays Wagner never did.

Casey Stengel
on Phil Rizzuto

Mickey Mantle. Outside of Babe Ruth, it was probably the best baseball name ever invented. His father picked the name, in honor of Mickey Cochrane, a Hall of Fame catcher for Detroit.

Mickey Herskowitz
author/sportswriter

Mantle was the last in a line of almost mythical New York Yankee sluggers who rose above their numbers and beyond the Hall of Fame: Babe Ruth, Lou Gehrig, Joe DiMaggio. He may have been the last true star who was not identified by the money he made.

Mickey Herskowitz

His fame, his legend, his popularity, seemed to rest not so much on what he achieved—and that was considerable—but on what he promised: a thrill with every at bat, power, speed, and the poetry of youth. . . . He played the game the way little kids did in their dreams.

Mickey Herskowitz
on Mickey Mantle

You'll never be a ballplayer. Take my advice, son, and forget baseball. Get into some other line of business.

Branch Rickey
*former St. Louis Cardinals and
Brooklyn Dodgers GM,
to Yogi Berra, after Berra's
unsuccessful tryout with the
Cardinals*

In recent years there has been a tendency to rate Yogi Berra as the second-best hitting catcher of the modern era—behind Johnny Bench. I have always found this comparison puzzling. Berra leads Bench in batting average by nearly 20 points as well as in RBIs and total runs scored, despite the fact that Yogi had fewer at-bats. Bench leads only in total home runs and ties Berra for total fielding average.

Phil Rizzuto

FAST FACT: Bench's mark for most career home runs by a catcher has since been surpassed by Mike Piazza.

Yogi Berra

NEW YORK YANKEES

No one feels baseball better than Yogi Berra, no one relishes the excitement of its competition more, no one reacts more quickly to its constant challenge. He is a masterpiece of a ballplayer.

Robert W. Creamer
historian/author

I played for Casey Stengel before and after he was a genius.

Warren Spahn
Hall of Fame pitcher sent to the minors by Stengel when both were with the Boston Braves in 1942. Spahn hooked up again with the Old Perfessor 23 years later as a New York Met

He was a brilliant strategist and could play the press the way Heifetz played the fiddle.

Maury Allen
on Casey Stengel

On the field he was a teacher. Off the field he was a talker.

Al Lopez

*onetime manager of both
the rival Cleveland Indians
and Chicago White Sox,
on Casey Stengel*

Casey Stengel had more baseball brains in his little finger than any other manager I knew had in their whole body.

Tommy Holmes

*Boston Braves player under
Stengel in 1942*

If there was any one great skill Casey had as a manager, it was knowing when to pick his spots. He didn't have a degree, but he was one of the greatest doctors of psychiatry I had ever seen.

Eddie Lopat

pitcher (1948–55)

I give the man a point for speed. I do this because Maris can run fast. Then I give him a point because he can slide fast. I give him another point because he can bunt. I also give him a point because he can field. He is very good around the fences—sometimes on top of the fences. Next, I give him a point because he can throw. A right fielder has to be a thrower or he's not a right fielder. So I add up my points, and I've got five for him before I even come to his hitting. I would say this is a good man.

Casey Stengel

I thought Roger Maris was the one guy we needed. He always played hard. And he would plow into second base with total abandon to break up a double play. He was a complete player and he could field and throw and run.

Whitey Ford

He's the only guy in baseball who can carry a club for a month. And the hell with what you hear. He hustles every minute on the field.

Thurman Munson
*catcher and Yankee captain
(1969–79),
on Reggie Jackson, before the
free-agent slugger signed with
New York*

Ron Guidry's the most impressive pitcher I've ever seen. He's more impressive than Tom Seaver or Jim Palmer or Nolan Ryan.

Sparky Lyle
pitcher (1972–78)

Ron Guidry was tougher on righties than lefties. That hard, hard slider looked like a low strike until the last minute, when it would break down and in on right-handers. He could make them look ridiculous with that pitch. And he had an up-and-away fastball. You're looking for that slider down, and you had no chance against that high fastball.

Rick Miller
12-year Boston Red Sox outfielder

Guidry possessed the best winning percentage of any 20-game winner in history.

Roger Kahn
author

NEW YORK YANKEES

Graig Nettles

The best all-around third baseman of the 1970s, probably the best defensive one ever, Graig Nettles had pop in his bat and also in his mouth.

Harvey Frommer
author

FAST FACT: Nettles smashed 20 home runs or more in eight of his 11 years as a Yankee. In 1976 he was the American League home run king

People recognize me wherever I go. . . . I was driving down the freeway in Los Angeles over the winter and a guy pulled up next to me and gave me the finger.

Graig Nettles
third base (1973–83)

What the Yankees need is a second-base coach.

Graig Nettles

His greatest asset is not his bat. It is his incredible ability to get rid of the ball. It sometimes seems that he throws it before he has caught it.

> ### *Newsday*
> *on Thurman Munson. The Yankee catcher batted .302 and was named AL Rookie of the Year in 1970*

He thought his job with the Yankees consisted of this one important thing: playing baseball hard, all the time. Walk up to the plate when the pain in the knees was like daggers. Make the throw to second base when the right arm was aching and useless. Run the bases like a fullback when one more collision might take him out for good.

> ### Mike Lupica
> New York Daily News,
> *on Thurman Munson*

He was simply the best late-season hitter who ever lived.

Earl Weaver
*Baltimore Orioles Hall of Fame manager,
on Reggie Jackson*

———

Championship teams keep following Reggie around.

Earl Weaver

———

I'm the straw that stirs the drink.

Reggie Jackson
right field (1977–81)

I think Reggie Jackson on your ball club is a part of a show of force. It's a show of power. I help to intimidate the opposition, just because I'm here. That's part of my role.

Reggie Jackson

The magnitude of me, the magnitude of the instance, the magnitude of New York—it's uncomfortable, it's miserable. It's uncomfortable being me, it's uncomfortable being recognized constantly, it's uncomfortable being considered something I'm not, an idol or a monster, something hated or loved.

Reggie Jackson

Ten or 20 years down the road, people will always associate Don Mattingly with the Yankees. With free agency, you don't have many players who are associated with teams anymore. But Donnie will always be remembered as a Yankee. . . . There are a few guys who, whether you're playing with them or against them, you root for them. He was one of those guys. People in baseball wanted Donnie to do well because of all he'd done and how he had done it.

Paul O'Neill

The kid is dynamite. I'm not sure if there's any ceiling for him.

Joe Torre

on shortstop Derek Jeter

———

Derek Jeter is a great player. He didn't have to prove it this Series. He could have taken it off and I still would have thought he was a great player.

Bobby Valentine

*former New York Mets manager,
after Jeter was named MVP of
the 2000 World Series*

———

All I've ever wanted to be is a Yankee. When I was a kid, I was always hoping there'd be a jersey left for me to wear with a single digit, because of all the retired numbers.

Derek Jeter

wearer of No. 2

NEW YORK YANKEES

Derek Jeter

I would certainly trade his World Series championship for this MVP trophy. That's the only reason I play baseball. It's what I'm consumed to do right now.

Alex Rodriguez
*who edged Boston's David Ortiz
for the 2005 AL MVP honor*

FAST FACT: Rodriguez is the first Yankee to win the award since Don Mattingly in 1985 and only the fourth player to win it with two teams (Barry Bonds: Pittsburgh and San Francisco; Jimmie Foxx: Philadelphia Athletics and Red Sox; and Frank Robinson: Cincinnati and Baltimore). A-Rod is also the fourth to win at two positions, along with Detroit's Hank Greenberg (first base and left field), the St. Louis Cardinals' Stan Musial (outfield and first base), and the Milwaukee Brewers' Robin Yount (shortstop and center field). The Yanks have won the award 19 times, the most of any team.

⸺◦⸺

The great thing is that he's always looking to improve. . . . We're talking about a guy who is Hall of Fame caliber.

Lou Piniella
*outfield (1974–84)/manager
(1986–87, 1988)
on A-Rod*

Alex Rodriguez

I can see they love Bernie here.

Robinson Cano

*second base (2005–),
after repeated ovations by the
sold-out crowd of 55,136 (raising
New York's home attendance
total to an American League-
record 4,090,696),on what
appeared to be Bernie Williams'
last game as a Yankee, Sept. 25,
2005—an 8–4 win over Toronto,
in which Williams went 1–for–4.
As events turned out, Williams,
who would have become an
unrestricted free agent after the
season, re-signed with New York
and will play a reduced role in
2006 after 15 seasons as the
Yankees' regular center fielder*

There's no reason you should ever doubt that guy. Ever.

Shawn Chacon

on ace closer Mariano Rivera

The one Yankee even the haters can't quite bring themselves to despise. . . . I think it's the vaguely elfin look about his eyes and ears. If you look at him long enough you can convince yourself that he isn't really of this earth, which makes his otherworldly postseason record completely reasonable.

Eric Neel
page Two, ESPN.com,
on Rivera

He's the best.

Jorge Posada
catcher (1995–),
on Rivera,
whose career postseason ERA
is an unheard-of .081 covering
111.7 innings, with 34 saves and
an 8–1 record through 2005

Mariano Rivera

NEW YORK YANKEES

It's really hard to center him. It's moving two ways, and it's moving pretty quickly. It's moving forward at 90-plus, and it's moving sideways rather late and rather quickly.

Bobby Valentine
on Mariano Rivera's legendary cutter

———

That's what you do in the postseason; you get it to Mo. You start checking off the innings and try to get him into the ball-game.

Jason Giambi
on Mariano Rivera

———

I trust him so much, because I know one thing, above anything else, whether it works or not, you know that he's going out there with the biggest heart in the world. He certainly doesn't shy away from the pressure.

Joe Torre
on Mariano Rivera

That impossible-to-detect break of the cutter, lasering in on a left-handed hitter so crazily . . . the Braves' Chipper Jones once likened it to "a buzz saw."

Bob Klapisch
ESPN.com,
on Mariano Rivera's money pitch

The feeling is that it's over. It doesn't always happen, but that's the feeling you have. Mo has been automatic for a while.

Derek Jeter
whenever Rivera enters a game

That he does what he does with one pitch is incredible. I mean, really, it's ridiculous. He makes it look easy.

Shawn Chacon
on Rivera

He's the Michael Jordan of baseball, one of the greatest baseball icons of the past 100 years.

Alex Rodriguez
on Mariano Rivera

It's not easy, but I trust my pitches and I trust my teammates behind me.

Mariano Rivera

To tell you the truth, I can't tell exactly why the cutter does what it does. When I first came up I threw the ball hard but it didn't move a lot. . . . So I just practiced with a lot of different grips until I found one that got the best movement.

Mariano Rivera

The kid throws too hard for us. He's too good for this league. I say we ban him from baseball.

Tom Kelly
former Minnesota Twins manager, on Rivera

I never thought I was going to get here. I was fired last year [St. Louis] and I thought that was my last stop. It's very emotional to finally get here. . . . I wish this feeling could last forever.

Joe Torre
after winning the 1996 World Series

I think Skip's the kind of guy who's going to go down with the guys that got him here. And as a player you love that.

Andy Pettitte
*pitcher (1995–2003),
on Joe Torre*

Joe lets players play and coaches coach.

Don Zimmer
coach (1995–2003)

His impact is all over this team. It's all over every player.

Darryl Strawberry
*outfield (1995–99),
on Joe Torre*

7

SHRINE TO NO. 7

So much enters into the making of the myth of Mickey Mantle. There was the always tantalizing "what if?" about his injury-plagued career: What could he have done on two good legs? Being a switch-hitter generated fabled overtones as well. The boyish good looks, shyness, and sonorous alliterative name also figured into the equation of the Commerce Comet as an American icon.

But likely the largest single factor contributing to his immense status was the Superman quality of his tape-measure home runs.

They say no one ever ripped the ball like Mantle, not even Ruth, who awed crowds with shocking displays of power. Mantle first staggered baseball followers with his monumental 565-foot blast off the Washington Senators' Chuck Stobbs in 1953 at Griffith Stadium, one of Mantle's favorite hitting grounds. The term "tape-measure home run" was coined in that instant.

The tale of the tape continued unabated in Mantle's Triple Crown year of 1956, when, on opening day, he again belted pitches clear out of Griffith Stadium, one in his first at-bat of the season and another in the sixth inning.

In the first game of a Memorial Day doubleheader that same year against Washington, at Yankee Stadium, where no fair ball had ever been hit out, Mantle walloped a Pedro Ramos pitch that slammed into the famed facade 117 feet above field level over the 344-foot sign in right. It came within 18 inches of escaping the stadium. Estimates say the ball would have traveled between 550 and 600 feet.

Detroit's Briggs Stadium was another preferred Mantle target, with four balls cannoned over the roof—the only player ever to accomplish that feat.

On the afternoon that the Yankees clinched their fifth American League pennant in six years—Sept. 18, 1956—Mantle clocked one over the left-centerfield roof in Chicago.

"It was the longest ball ever hit at Comiskey Park," said Mantle. "They measured it at 550 feet. Now that the Sox have played their last game there, that's one record I can be sure will never be surpassed."

It is one of baseball's landmark home runs. . . . If it has kinship in baseball history, it is with Ruth's "called shot" in the 1932 World Series; but where Ruth's clout crowned a legend, Mantle's was the launching of one. Of all the fabled home runs in baseball history, Mantle's alone stands for something other than dramatic victory. This particular cannon shot stands for might and power; it is its own colossal symbol.

Donald Honig
on Mantle's 565-foot home run, April 17, 1953, Griffith Stadium, Washington, D.C.

He came so close to making history that he made it.

Robert W. Creamer
on Mantle's shot that nearly cleared the right-field facade of Yankee Stadium, May 30, 1956

At Griffith Stadium in Washington, D.C., Mantle, batting right-handed against Washington lefty Chuck Stobbs, hit a rising line drive that left the playing field at the 391-foot mark. It grazed the 60-foot beer sign on top of the football scoreboard behind the bleachers, carried across Fifth Street, and landed in a backyard on Oakdale Street. Yankees publicity director Red Patterson immediately dashed out of the press box, left the stadium, and found the spot where witnesses said the ball had landed. Then he paced off the distance and fixed it at 565 feet. . . . Later the Senators marked the spot on the beer sign where the ball had left the park. Though Mantle probably hit longer home runs, the 565-footer still stands as the longest hit ever measured.

Lonnie Wheeler
author

He hit balls over buildings.

Casey Stengel

New York Yankees

Mickey Mantle

Nobody's half as good as Mickey Mantle.

Al Kaline

Detroit Tigers Hall of Fame
right fielder,
in reply to a fan who had taunted
the Tiger great by saying he
wasn't half as good as Mantle

More than 25,000 men have been skilled enough to grace a major-league diamond. Only a handful of them, perhaps five or six at most, can claim they were as accomplished as the Commerce Comet. Ballplayers continue to grow bigger, faster, stronger, yet not one has been able to match Mantle's combination of tape-measure power and Olympian speed.

Richard Lally

author

Mickey tried to hit every one like they didn't count under 400 feet.

Casey Stengel

One of these days, he'll hit the ball so hard, it'll burst and all he'll get for his efforts will be a single.

Casey Stengel

They hung the nickname "the Commerce Comet" on him, except he was faster than a comet. Fastest thing I ever saw.

Tom Sturdivant
pitcher (1955–59)

This kid runs so fast in the outfield, he doesn't bend a blade of grass.

Casey Stengel
on the speed of Mickey Mantle

If I could run like Mantle, I'd hit .400 every year!

Ted Williams

What can you say after you have said how great he was?

> **Gene Woodling**
> *outfield (1949–54),*
> *on Mickey Mantle*

———

The body of a god. Only his legs are mortal.

> **Jerry Coleman**
> *second base (1949–57)*

———

With his one good leg, he could outrun everyone.

> **Gene Woodling**

———

There has never been anyone like this kid. He has more speed than any slugger, and more slug than any speedster.

> **Casey Stengel**
> *on The Mick*

No man in the history of baseball had as much power as Mickey Mantle. No man. You're not talking about ordinary power. Dave Kingman had power. Willie Mays had power. Then when you're talking about Mantle—it's an altogether different level.

Billy Martin

Mickey had more raw talent than any player I'd ever seen, and he also had good baseball sense. . . . Great base-running instincts. Faster than Mays, Rickey Henderson, Lou Brock, all those guys, and he knew what to do with it, too.

Frank Crosetti
shortstop (1932–48)/
coach (1946–68)

Willie Mays and I, we broke in together in 1951 and then the big question was, "Who's the best, Willie, Mick, or the Duke?" I always said, long before Henry Aaron broke Ruth's home run record, that Hank was the best ballplayer of our era. He was doing the same thing Willie and I were doing. He just wasn't doing it in New York.

Mickey Mantle

Mantle once said that every time he swung the bat, he was swinging for a home run.

Lonnie Wheeler

8

PINSTRIPE HUMOR

These days baseball is different. You come to spring training, you get your legs ready, your arms loose, your agents ready, your lawyers lined up.

Dave Winfield
outfield (1981–90)

He'd fall in a sewer and come up with a gold watch.

Casey Stengel
on Yogi Berra

―――――

Reggie Jackson is a lot like Mantle. They think a 380-foot homer doesn't count. They both tried to hit the ball 500 feet.

Joe DiMaggio

―――――

There will be no Derek Jeter Center after all. New York attorney Kerry Konrad won the right in an eBay auction to name Boston's FleetCenter for a day. For his $2,325, Konrad wanted to honor the New York Yankees shortstop. But FleetCenter officials rejected the name.

Darren Rovell
ESPN.com

I had no idea that this joke would get so much attention. I've had my laugh. But I could have made it much worse, like the A-Rod Center, Bucky Dent Center, the Aaron Boone Center, or the "Only 25 More [championships] To Go" Center. . . . I'm sure if [Yankees owner] George Steinbrenner were foolish enough to auction off the naming rights to Yankee Stadium for a day, Red Sox fans would have thought of something clever.

Kerry Konrad
eBay auction winner,
whose "Derek Jeter Center"
submission made the FleetCenter's
president and chief executive
"afraid of the volume of phone calls
bogging down our switchboard,
the number of e-mails clogging our
portal, and the potential graffiti on
the side of our building."

He needed an oxygen tank there. It was kind of funny to watch.

Derek Jeter

*on Jorge Posada scoring from
first in an early September 2005
win over Boston, in which two
Red Sox errors on a routine
single encouraged the slow-
chugging Bombers catcher
to motor for extra bases*

The Yankees soaked another clubhouse floor and walls with sprayed bubbly. They've won so many of these things (eight consecutive division titles and counting) they could conduct a seminar on proper cork-popping technique.

Gene Wojciechowski

*writer, ESPN.com,
after the Yankees claimed the
AL East crown outright at
Fenway Park in the 161st
game of the 2005 season*

You're my closer. Don't start sweating bullets if you give up a couple of hits. I gave up more than 2,500 myself.

Bob Lemon

manager (1978–79, 1981–82), to first-year-Yankee closer Goose Gossage in July 1978. Lemon was well qualified to speak, having been a seven-time All-Star hurler with Cleveland from the mid-1940s through the late '50s, winning 20 games seven times and totaling 207 victories over his 13 major-league seasons, all with the Indians

Baseball is such a nice, simple, children's game. It's a shame adults have to complicate it and screw things up.

Bob Lemon

After watching Lou Piniella for a time, someone described him as "the best slow outfielder in baseball."

Roger Kahn

They say he's funny. Well, he has a lovely wife and family, a beautiful home, money in the bank, and he plays golf with millionaires. What's funny about that?

Casey Stengel
on Yogi Berra

———

I thought it was the ball.

Roger Clemens
on throwing Mike Piazza's splintered bat back at the Mets' batter during Game Two of the 2000 World Series

———

It's got to be better than rooming with Joe Page.

Joe DiMaggio
on marriage with Marilyn Monroe

———

The Goose should do more pitching and less quacking.

George Steinbrenner
on reliever Goose Gossage

This [bleep] don't count. This [bleep] don't go on the bubble-gum card.

Rickey Henderson
outfield (1985–89),
on spring training

———

The wind was blowin' about a hundred degrees.

Mickey Rivers
center field (1976–79)

———

My goals are to hit .300, score 100 runs, and stay injury-prone.

Mickey Rivers

———

He'd give you the shirt off his back. Of course, he'd call a press conference to announce it.

Jim "Catfish" Hunter
on Reggie Jackson

No one hit home runs the way the Babe did. They were like homing pigeons. The ball would leave the bat, pause briefly, suddenly gain its bearings, then take off for the stands.

Lefty Gómez
pitcher (1930–42)

When it comes down to it, there's only one day a year when we allow ourselves to get giddy—the parade.

Bernie Williams

We've got a problem here. Luis Tiant wants to use the bathroom and it says no foreign objects in the toilet.

Graig Nettles

Don Zimmer's face looks like a blocked punt.

Joe Garagiola
nine-year major-league catcher/longtime TV broadcaster, on the former Yankees coach

9

GREAT
MOMENTS

Jack Chesbro's 41-victory season in 1904, the Babe's 60 home runs in 1927, Gehrig's four homers against the Athletics in '32, Dodger catcher Mickey Owen's passed-ball error in the '41 Series that enabled Tommy Henrich to reach first and keep a winning Yankee drive alive, Don Larsen's perfect game in '56 (the same year as Mantle's triple crown), Roger Maris's 61 home runs in '61, Reggie Jackson's homer clinic in the '77 Series, Bucky Dent's home run against the Red Sox in the '78 AL playoff game, the perfect games of David Wells and David Cone in '98 and '99 respectively, the incredible world-championship run of the late-20th-century Bombers . . .

The Yankees have been involved in more immortal moments than the rest of baseball combined. Savor a handful of history, Yankees-style.

Thirty thousand gasped, according to the press. Its length was not determined—the tape measure, like air-conditioning, awaited invention—but this one, to center field, was so extravagant that Cleveland catcher Joe Sewell demanded the umpires check Ruth's bat, arguing that no mortal could hit a ball that far without the aid of lead in the weapon. The umpires dutifully went over the bludgeon and concluded what all the world knew. It wasn't the bat. It was Ruth.

John Mosedale

on what was regarded as the second-longest home run ever hit by Babe Ruth, in a 6–4 victory over Cleveland in June 1927

The Babe made his triumphant, almost regal tour of the bases. He jogged around slowly, touched each base firmly, and when he embedded his spikes in the rubber disk to record officially Homer 60, hats were tossed in the air, papers were torn up and tossed crazily, and the spirit of celebration permeated the place.

New York Times
Oct. 1, 1927

They could no more have stopped Babe Ruth from hitting that home run that gave him a new world record than you could have stopped a locomotive by sticking your foot in front of it. Once he had that 59th, that Number 60 was as sure as the rising sun. A more determined athlete than George Herman Ruth never lived.

Paul Gallico
New York Daily News,
Oct. 1, 1927

It was the second four-game sweep in [World] Series history, the only other being the Braves' triumph over the 1914 Athletics. . . . In 1932 and in 1938 the Yankees swept the Cubs; in 1939, the Reds; and in 1950, the Phillies. Those were sweeps. There were six other Yankee world championships between 1927 and 1950.

John Mosedale

on New York's sweep of Pittsburgh in the 1927 World Series

I took the two most expensive aspirins in history.

Wally Pipp

first base (1915–25)

FAST FACT: Accounts vary on exactly what caused Pipp to have to sit out a game on June 1, 1925. Theories include the well-known "headache" speculation and also that he was hit in the head during batting practice prior to the game's start. Regardless, he was replaced by a youngster named Lou Gehrig, who went on to play in 2,130 consecutive games; Pipp never made it back into the New York lineup.

The Babe was a boisterous, big-hearted child of nature who exuded color out of every pore. He was a legend come to life. Paul Bunyan in the flesh. ... . No one but Babe would have dared to point to the bleachers where he would then hit a home run off Charlie Root in the 1932 World Series.

Arthur Daley
New York Times

I didn't exactly point to any spot. All I wanted to do was give the thing a ride out of the park. I used to pop off a lot about hitting homers.

Babe Ruth
right field (1920–34),
to Chicago sportswriter
John Carmichael,
about his famous "called-shot"
home run off the Cubs' Charlie
Root in the 1932 World Series

If I'm having this much trouble with this pitch, maybe Mickey is, too.

> **Tommy Henrich**
> *right field (1937–50),*
> *on his legendary third-out*
> *strikeout that got away from*
> *Dodgers catcher Mickey Owen*
> *with two outs in the ninth in*
> *Game Four of the 1941 World*
> *Series. Owen's passed ball led*
> *to a four-run Yankees rally and*
> *a 7–4 win*

What if Martin don't catch Rob-A-Son's fly ball, which he did splendidly.

> **Casey Stengel**
> *on Billy Martin's dashing game-*
> *and series-saving infield catch*
> *of Jackie Robinson's bases-*
> *loaded pop-up in the seventh*
> *inning of Game Seven of the*
> *1952 World Series to preserve*
> *a 4–2 New York victory over*
> *Brooklyn*

He will think about it every day for the rest of his life, just like I do.

Don Larsen
*pitcher (1955–59) of the only perfect game in World Series history,
on David Wells's perfecto in 1998*

⚊⚌⚊

My top memory was Don Larsen's perfect game in 1956. Next was Reggie Jackson's three homers in the final game of 1977.

Bob Sheppard
New York's legendary "Voice of God" public address announcer since 1951

I can remember it clear as a bell. "Pinch-hitting, No. 8, Dale Mitchell." At that moment, my mother put her arm around me and said, "Don't tell anyone this is your dad, 'cause if he gets a hit, these fans might kill us." That made me realize that this was something important.

Bo Mitchell

whose father, Dale, was the last out in Don Larsen's perfect game in the 1956 World Series

What if the ball don't hit him in the throat, dontcha think we win it and I'm out with a championship even though I'm discharged?

Casey Stengel

FAST FACT: In the eighth inning, a ground ball bounced up and hit shortstop Tony Kubek in the throat during Game Seven of the 1960 World Series. The Pirates scored five runs in that inning to take a two-run lead into the ninth. The Yankees managed to get two in the top half to tie it, but this Series will always be remembered for Bill Mazeroski's bottom-of-the-ninth World Series-winning home run. It would be the last game Stengel managed for the Yankees after recording 10 pennants and seven world championships in his 12 years at the New York helm.

The essential difference between Ruth and Maris was not merely that Maris was a better all-around ballplayer, but that Maris had to worry about Ruth and Ruth didn't have to worry about Maris.

James Reston
New York Times

One guy wrote that I don't deserve to break Ruth's record. Now Ruth, he was the greatest. But what am I supposed to do, stop hitting homers? They make it sound as if I'd be committing a sin if I broke the record.

Roger Maris
right field (1960–66)

Maris was never treated as a champion because he challenged the immortals, and won.

Mickey Mantle

I saw it was a good fastball. I was ready and I connected. As soon as I hit it, I knew it was number 61; it was the only time that the number of the homer ever flashed into my mind as I hit it. Then I heard the tremendous roar of the crowd. I could see them all standing. Then my mind went blank.

Roger Maris

I knew he hit the stuff out of it, but I didn't think it was going to be a home run. I turned around and then saw the thing going way up. I give Roger all the credit in the world. I gave him what I feel was my best fastball and he hit it.

Tracy Stallard
Boston Red Sox pitcher of record on Maris's 61st home run

Whether I beat Ruth's record or not is for others to say. But it gives me a wonderful feeling to know that I'm the only man in history to hit 61 home runs. Nobody can take that away from me. Babe Ruth was a big man in baseball, maybe the biggest ever. I'm not saying I am of his caliber, but I'm glad to say I hit more than he did in a season.

Roger Maris

Commissioner Ford Frick attached an asterisk next to the 61 homers in the record book because Roger Maris failed to hit them in the first 154 games, which happened to be the schedule when Ruth got the 60. I thought it was a ridiculous ruling. It made no sense at all. Check further and you'll note that the same year, 1961, Sandy Koufax broke Christy Mathewson's National League strikeout record. Mathewson set it in 1903, when they played a 140-game schedule. But you won't find an asterisk attached to Koufax.

Mickey Mantle

In May 1963, batting against Bill Fischer of the Kansas City Athletics, Mickey Mantle hit what may have been the longest home run ever . In the bottom of the 11th inning, Mantle connected with all of his might. He said that it was the only time in his life that he actually saw the bat bend in his hands when he made contact. It sent Fischer's pitch on an incredibly high, straight line toward the right-field roof at Yankee Stadium. By the accounts of those present, the ball was still rising when it struck the facade of the roof. One scientist estimated the drive would have traveled a minimum of 620 feet.

Lonnie Wheeler

I must admit, when Reggie hit his third home run and I was sure nobody was looking, I applauded in my glove.

Steve Garvey

former Los Angeles Dodgers
first baseman,
on Reggie Jackson's three
consecutive home runs in Game
Six of the 1977 World Series

I had gone up to the plate looking to drive the ball for extra bases . The moment I hit the pitch I ran my tail off. I figured it was off the wall and I was hoping to hustle to second with the lead run. I didn't find out I had hit a home run until I had passed first base and saw the umpire's signal.

Bucky Dent

shortstop (1977–82),
on his epic homer off Boston's
Mike Torrez in the 1978 AL
Playoff at Fenway Park, won by
New York, 5–4

I really didn't know whether it went over the wall or not.

Jeffrey Meier

> *FAST FACT:* The 12-year-old Meier's in-the-field-of-play catch of Derek Jeter's eighth-inning fly ball to right in the opening game of the 1996 American League Championship Series against the Baltimore Orioles was ruled a game-tying home run by Umpire Rich Garcia. The Yanks went on to win it, 5–4, in the 11th on a homer by Bernie Williams.

Me and the kid almost touched gloves. It was a routine fly ball. In my mind, there is no way in the world I would have dropped it. Merlin must have been in the air.

Tony Tarasco

Baltimore Orioles right fielder, on the infamous catch by Yankees "angel in the outfield" Jeffrey Meier

My last comment to him leaving the bull-pen was, "Don't just throw because your stuff is good. Concentrate on your pitches, because your stuff is so outstanding."

Mel Stottlemyre

to David Wells, just prior to his 4–0 perfect-game win against Minnesota, May 17, 1998

I think it's time for you to break out your knuckleball.

David Cone

to David Wells as the left-hander took the mound for the eighth inning of his perfect game

FAST FACT: The comment cracked up Wells. Later he credited Cone's remark as a key to helping him stay loose for the tension-packed last two innings.

To pitch a perfect game wearing pinstripes at Yankee Stadium, it's unbelievable.

David Wells

pitcher (1997–98, 2002–03)

It is the happiest day of my life. The way I did this is unbelievable. I don't know how to explain it. Today, they gave me a chance to come through . It's a dream come true.

Luis Sojo
infield (1996–99, 2000–01, 2003), on his 2000 World Series-winning hit up the middle that gave the Yankees their 26th world title

The biggest game I ever pitched was when I jumped on a raft and left Cuba.

Orlando Hernández

If there's a turning point in the season, this should be it. This is incredible, especially this late in the game. I've never seen anything like this.

Bernie Williams

on the 20–11 win over Tampa Bay, June 21, 2005, which featured a phenomenal 17-run Yankees turnaround in the bottom of the eighth, matching the largest victory after trailing by eight runs in major-league history. Behind Williams (five RBIs) and Gary Sheffield (seven RBIs), the Yankees exploded for 13 runs in the big inning, including consecutive homers by Sheffield, Alex Rodriguez, and Hideki Matsui. Making the win all the more bizarre was the Devil Rays' pounding of Randy Johnson for seven runs in just three innings. It was the Big Unit's shortest outing in five years

It was the fifth time in franchise history the Yankees led off a game with back-to-back homers, the first since Alfonso Soriano and Derek Jeter at the Mets on June 28, 2003.

Associated Press

after Jeter and second baseman Robinson Cano led off a 5–0 triumph over Toronto, Sept. 23, 2005

In Joe Torre's 10-year Bronx tenure, the Yankees have never had to work harder for a division title. Injuries . . . the Red Sox . . . the constant, sometimes-suffocating pressure that comes with wearing pinstripes all made for a celebration to remember in the cramped—and wet—visitors' clubhouse at Fenway.

Gene Wojciechowski

after the Yankees claimed the 2005 AL East title outright in the second-to-last game of 2005

The record is certainly something I'll think about once this whole thing is over.

Alex Rodriguez

on his record-breaking 47th home run, Sept. 28, 2005, breaking Joe DiMaggio's club mark of 46 homers in a single season by a right-handed batter, set by the Clipper in 1937. Rodriguez's smash ignited a Yanks' comeback that resulted in a critical 2–1 victory over Baltimore, putting New York up by one game over Boston in the AL East race with four games to go

The whole game was a grinder, we did a lot of things well. It doesn't mean anything if we don't go out there and play the way we're supposed to.

Jorge Posada

who beat the tag at home for the Yanks' go-ahead run in the seventh inning of New York's 3–2 win over the Los Angeles Angels in Game Four of the 2005 ALDS, tying the series at two games apiece. Following Shawn Chacon's two-run, four-hit mound performance over 6⅓ innings, Mariano Rivera closed out the final six outs without a hit

That's a tough play. And it's just one play.

Derek Jeter

on Adam Kennedy's second-inning deep fly between center-fielder Bubba Crosby and right-fielder Gary Sheffield in the fifth and deciding game of the 2005 ALDS that caused a collision between the two Yankee outfielders. The costly play allowed two Angels runs to score. Los Angeles took the lead, and soon after, the series

If Sheff hadn't been there, Bubba would have caught it. If Bubba hadn't been there, Sheff would have caught it. It was just in the right place.

Mike Mussina

pitcher (2001–),
on the above-mentioned Crosby-Sheffield collision that figured critically in the 2005 ALDS Game Five loss to Los Angeles

10

THE GREAT YANKEE TEAMS

Yankees manager Miller Huggins once said: "A team is like a bridge hand. You've got to get up your strongest suit."

It's safe to say the Yanks have won their share of bridge hands over the years. They've also crossed a few bridges, for no team in professional sports history has ever strung together so many championship titles: 39 American League flags and 26 World Series crowns.

Who was the best? The 1927 Murderers' Row team, the DiMaggio-led Bombers of '39, the '61 powerhouse led by the M&M boys, the Reggie Jackson-led Yanks of '77, or the end-of-the-century New Yorkers who took four world titles in five years?

There may never be agreement on that one.

The Yankees rose in 1927 to a peak which many believe they have never surpassed. This, they say, was the team. Greater than any that had gone before, greater than any that has followed.

Frank Graham

The Yankees took off like one of Ruth's home runs, neither failing nor falling, roaring off on opening day and never looking back, never falling from first place. This can be regarded as dull or seen as something marvelous to behold, like a [Franklin D.] Roosevelt presidential campaign, or Joe Louis touching someone up, or the Marx Brothers.

John Mosedale
on the 1927 Yankees

Ruth, the greatest ballplayer who ever lived. Combs, a star of the first magnitude. Meusel, the greatest thrower who ever lived. The three of them and Lazzeri each knocked in 100 runs that year. Gehrig, a superstar, one of the greatest. Lazzeri, a star, a great thrower, good hitter. Koenig, erratic but he made it up with his hitting. Dugan. Ah, one of the lesser lights, but yes, I'll go for this: I could field as well as anybody in those days. The catching, ordinary. Hoyt, a star. Pennock, a star. Pipgras, a good pitcher. Moore, the best relief pitcher I ever saw.

Joe Dugan
on the '27 Yankees

They don't just beat you, they break your heart.

Joe Judge
Washington Senators
first baseman (1915–32),
on the 1927 Yankees

Writers who saw the 1927 team know that subsequent years have not seen its equal.

Dan Daniel
longtime New York sportswriter

History, like life, is unfair, and the 1927 team is remembered for scoring the most runs, not for giving up the fewest.

John Mosedale

I certainly have no desire to say anything about the pitchers of 1927, but I believe that the hurlers of today are throwing more varieties than the 1927 gang did.

Joe DiMaggio
1961

The 1927 Yankees probably beat them-selves less than any ball club that ever lived.

Waite Hoyt

In the 1939 Series, Joe McCarthy's Yanks clobbered the Reds 4–0 to win an unprece-dented fourth straight World Champion-ship. . . . Not McGraw's Giants, not Connie Mack's A's, not even Huggins's Yankees—no one had ever accomplished that feat.

John Tullius
author/writer

We'd hit the home run, yes, but it was a team of players that played the game right and knew how to play it.

Tony Kubek
on the 1961 Yankees

We're the best team money can't buy, and they're the best team money can buy. They have a lot of players who play their best under pressure.

George Brett
Kansas City Royals Hall of Famer, on the 1978 Yankees

Whoever first proclaimed the mantra, "There is no 'I' in Team," was a better speller than a thinker. . . . The New York Yankees' championship teams of 1977 and '78 would certainly hold the record, if such records were kept, for the greatest number of clashing egos on a single ball club.

Roger Kahn

Conflict is the stuff of drama. With the 1978 Yankees, you also find a time that many believed, and many still believe a quarter of a century later, was the Yankee season nonpareil.

Roger Kahn

There wasn't a Murderers' Row; there was no Bambino. It was all about being a team.

Jay David

*on the 1996 world-champion
New York Yankees*

———

They're not intimidating. It's not like they're sending up Murderers' Row, but they get hits when they have to get hits.

Bobby Valentine

on the 1998 Yankees

———

I never saw the '27 Yankees or the '39 Yankees, but I did see the Oakland A's of the early '70s and Cincinnati's Big Red Machine, and this is the best team I've ever seen.

Joe Torre

on the record-setting 1998 Yanks

We don't have one big guy. We have a team full of big guys.

Tim Raines

outfield/designated hitter
(1996–98),
on the 1998 world champions

———

You don't win 114 games by being lucky.

Mike Hargrove

former Cleveland Indians manager,
on the 1998 Bombers

———

I think we can hold up to one of those great teams because of what we have accomplished. I think our run of five postseasons is pretty damn good. With free agency and players changing teams so often, to be able to find ourselves here again is a pretty good run. I think our ball club should be right up there with any of the clubs that have put something together.

Joe Torre

on his 2000 world champs

I will say this, I don't know if any other team in New York has ever done any better.

George Steinbrenner
on the 2000 New York Yankees

———

They may say it's the greatest team ever, but you'll get arguments from the great Yankee teams—the '27 Yankees, the Yankee teams that won five World Series in a row (1949–53). But absolutely, I think you have an argument for this being the greatest team.

Reggie Jackson
on the 2000 Yanks

———

What I probably most admire and am most proud of with this team is their resolve and grittiness.

Joe Torre
on the 2000 club

We may not have the best players, but we certainly have the best team.

Joe Torre
on the 2000 Bronx Bombers

⊸⊸⊸

This team never will be confused with the great pinstripers of past lore, the ballclubs of Ruth, Gehrig, DiMaggio or Mantle. But it will be remembered as a group of low-key pros led by their redoubtable manager.

Jon Saraceno
on the 2000 Yanks

⊸⊸⊸

They seem like they just pound on you. You don't get a reprieve even with the number six, seven, eight, or nine hitters. Normally, you get an out or two down there.

Al Leiter
pitcher (2005)/former New York Mets pitcher, on the bottom half of the 2000 Yankees lineup

This is a group of 25 MVPs. Every game there is a new hero.

Derek Jeter
2000 World Series MVP

━━◦○◦━━

These guys had a team concept that was tremendous. I've had better teams, but none with a bigger heart.

George Steinbrenner
on the 2000 world champions

━━◦○◦━━

They knew how to do it because they've done it before. They told themselves they're a great team—and believed it. They knew the map, the road they had to follow. . . . Put the emphasis on team. This is one of the all-time great baseball teams. If you talk about great individuals and superstars, this team doesn't finish high.

Reggie Jackson
on the 2000 Yanks

After a season like no other in their remarkable history, the 2001 Yankees will be remembered for something more: for what they gave their city, for the moments they won back from despair.

Glenn Stout

We're taking every game like it's October, because it is for us.

Alex Rodriguez
*during the final week of the 2005
regular season, leading Boston
by a half game with six games
remaining*

This team is resilient. We don't quit.

Gary Sheffield
on the 2005 Yanks

The mark of a team isn't winning the championship; it's how you defend the championship.

George Steinbrenner

11

NEW YORK YANKEES ALL-TIME TEAM

*P*ick an all-time New York Yankees team?

Naturally, we'll offend some—maybe many. But there'll be none of that pussy-footing "move Mantle to right to make room for DiMag in center" low-rent cowardice here. With the nerve of a demolitions expert, it's one person per position—no second-place consolations. And forget about that messy designated hitter business, too.

Envision the classic tones of Yankees public-address legend Bob Sheppard announcing this lineup in the cavernous reverberation of the old Yankee Stadium.

"Your attention, please, ladies and gentlemen —now batting for the Yankees . . ."

LOU GEHRIG
First base (1923–39)

Seven-time AL All-Star
Two-time AL MVP (1927, '36)
AL Triple Crown winner (1934)
Three-time AL home run king (1931, '34, '36)
Five-time AL RBI champion (1927–28, 1930–31, '34)
Hall of Fame (1939)

Kid, that was the greatest I ever seen.

Babe Ruth
to Lou Gehrig, June 3, 1932, after Gehrig slammed four consecutive home runs against the Philadelphia Athletics—a feat Ruth never achieved—and was robbed of a fifth on a great catch by Al Simmons

---

What visions burn, what dreams possess him, the seeker of the night. The packed stands of the stadium, the bleachers sweltering with their unshaded hordes, the faultless velvet of the diamond. The mounting roar of 80,000 voices and Gehrig coming to bat.

Thomas Wolfe
author, You Can't Go Home Again

TONY LAZZERI
Second base (1926–37)

1933 AL All-Star
Hall of Fame (1991)

⎯⎯⎯

That young Eyetalian is a ballplayer. When things get tough over there, the others don't look to Ruth or any of the other veterans. They look to Lazzeri.

Timmy Connelly
*American League umpire,
one month after Tony Lazzeri
joined the Yankees in 1926*

⎯⎯⎯

He taught us what it meant to be a Yankee.

Lefty Gómez
on Tony Lazzeri

GRAIG NETTLES
Third base (1973–83)

Five-time AL All-Star
Two-time Gold Glove Award winner (1977–78)
AL Extra Base Hits leader (1976)

—◦—

That was one of the greatest exhibitions of playing third base I've seen in all my career.

Tommy Lasorda
former Los Angeles Dodgers manager,
on Graig Nettles's outstanding performance in Game Three of the 1978 World Series. It is estimated that Nettles saved five runs on his diving, twisting stops of blistering smashes in the third, fifth, and sixth innings—twice when the bases were loaded.

—◦—

He dives, makes unbelievable plays, half in defense of his life, half just in defense.

Sparky Lyle

DEREK JETER
Shortstop (1995–)

Six-time AL All-Star
1996 AL Rookie of the Year
2000 Major League All-Star Game MVP
2000 World Series MVP

—◊—

Derek Jeter is the kind of player, who one day I will get to say, "I played with him."

Paul O'Neill

—◊—

He's our Gibraltar.

Joe Torre
on Yankee captain Derek Jeter

—◊—

When I come back, I want to come back as Derek Jeter.

George Steinbrenner

YOGI BERRA
Catcher (1946–63)

15-time consecutive AL All-Star (1948–62)
Three-time AL MVP (1951, 1954–55)
Hall of Fame (1972)

———

Strange things happen to the reputations of players after they retire. Yogi was always kind of a funny-looking little guy; he looked like if he was a piece of furniture you'd sand him off some. Joe Garagiola spent all those years telling funny stories about the kind of dopey stuff Yogi used to say and do. Gradually, the image of Yogi as a kind of short, knobby, comic-book reader grew larger and larger, and the memory of Yogi Berra as one hell of a catcher drooped into the background.

Bill James
historian/author

———

You couldn't pitch to him. He had no weaknesses. He was the most dangerous hitter ever.

Jerry Coleman

BOB MEUSEL
Left field (1920–29)
AL home run, RBI, extra base hits
champion (1925)

Forty years later [Waite] Hoyt wondered why [Bob] Meusel was not in the Hall of Fame. "He was as good a ballplayer as I've ever seen," said the teammate of Ruth and Gehrig, the foe of Cobb and Speaker, the observer of Mays and Mantle.

John Mosedale

Meusel's arm was the best I ever saw. And I'm talking about strong arms, not merely accurate ones. Meusel threw strikes to any base from the outfield.

Bob Quinn
*former Boston Red Sox/
Atlanta Braves president*

JOE DIMAGGIO
Center field (1936–42, 1946–51)

13-time AL All-Star
Three-time AL MVP (1939, '41, '47)
Two-time AL batting champion (1939–40)
Two-time AL home run champion (1937, '48)
Two-time AL RBI champion (1941, '48)
Hall of Fame (1955)

Joe DiMaggio is the best all-around player I've ever seen.

Mickey Mantle

Joe did everything so naturally that half the time he gave the impression he wasn't trying. He made the rest of them look like plumbers.

Casey Stengel

Joe's a man who was meant to play ball on hot afternoons on the grass of big cities. He never belonged in the rain.

Jimmy Cannon
sportswriter

BABE RUTH
Right field (1920–34)

Two-time AL All-Star
AL MVP (1923)
AL batting champion (1924)
12-time AL home run king
Six-time AL RBI champion
11-time AL leader, walks
13-time AL leader, slugging percentage
Hall of Fame (1936)

Ruth won for baseball the number one position in American sport. He did it all with a large bat, a homely face, a warming charm, a bad boy complex, an inherent love for his fellow man, an almost legendary indifference to convention and a personal magnetism more irresistible than the flute to the cobra.

Waite Hoyt

There will never be another guy like the Babe. I get more kick from seeing him hit one than I do from hitting one myself.

Lou Gehrig

WHITEY FORD
Pitcher (1950, 1953–67)

Eight-time AL All-Star
Cy Young Award winner (1961)
Three-time *Sporting News* Pitcher of the Year
(1955, '61, '63)
Two-time AL ERA leader (1956, '58)
Three-time AL leader, wins (1955, '61, '63)
Hall of Fame (1974)

Whitey was a master. It was like watching a pitching textbook in the flesh.

Ralph Terry
pitcher (1956–57, 1959–64)

If the World Series was on the line and I could pick one pitcher, I'd choose Whitey Ford every time.

Mickey Mantle

CASEY STENGEL
Manager (1949–60)

Seven world championships
10 American League pennants
Hall of Fame (1966)

―――――

Keep your eyes off the scoreboard. Keep them on your own game. Pay attention to your own game.

Casey Stengel

―――――

I never saw a man who juggled his lineup so much and who played so many hunches so successfully.

Connie Mack
Philadelphia Athletics manager (1901–50),
on Casey Stengel

NEW YORK YANKEES ALL-TIME TEAM

Lou Gehrig, *First base*

Tony Lazzeri, *Second base*

Graig Nettles, *Third base*

Derek Jeter, *Shortstop*

Yogi Berra, *Catcher*

Bob Meusel, *Left field*

Joe DiMaggio, *Center field*

Babe Ruth, *Right field*

Whitey Ford, *Pitcher*

Casey Stengel, *Manager*

12

FIELDS
OF PLAY

Yankee Stadium is a law unto itself. . . . I once sneaked out to center field as a youth to see how things looked from Mickey Mantle's point of view and felt the same tingle some people get from Civil War battlefields.

Wilfrid Sheed
author

The House That Ruth Built.

Fred G. Lieb
legendary sportswriter who coined the timeless nickname in 1923

The old Hilltoppers' ballpark was located on a north Manhattan hillside, at Broadway and 162nd Street. My cousin and I went to [our] very first game in 1903. We sat in the bleachers. It rained and, due to inexperience, the front office hadn't provided for rain checks and made an announcement that anyone present could get in free the next day. Of course, everyone in New York turned up, claiming they'd been there when it rained, and there was a riot.

Dan Daniel

With a touch of lèse majesté, and perhaps avarice, the Giants allowed the American League club to share the Polo Grounds, beginning in 1913, by which time they were called the Yankees, a name given them by Jim Price, sports editor of the *New York Press*, because it fit more easily into headlines.

John Mosedale

If you had to limit yourself to one aspect of American life, the showdowns between pitcher and hitter, quarterback and defense, hustler and fish, would tell you more about politics, manners, style in this country than any other one thing. Sports constitute a code, a language of the emotions, and a tourist who skips the stadiums will not recoup his losses at Lincoln Center or Grant's Tomb.

Wilfrid Sheed

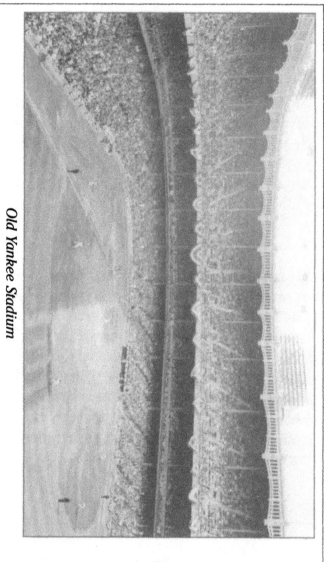

Old Yankee Stadium

NATIONAL BASEBALL HALL OF FAME LIBRARY, COOPERSTOWN, N.Y.

I'd give a year of my life if I can hit a home run in the first game in this new park.

Babe Ruth

who clouted a third-inning three-run home run on Opening Day at Yankee Stadium, April 18, 1923, in a 4–1 win over the Red Sox

The cathedral that is Yankee Stadium belongs to a Chapel.

Vin Scully

legendary Dodgers broadcaster

There are ghosts here and a rich tradition. You can sense it all around you. It's not just an invention of the press. . . . In my office there's a picture of Gehrig behind my desk. I inherited it, but I wouldn't think of removing it. That's what the stadium is all about.

Joe Torre

Gehrig liked to hit in the arena on the east bank of the Harlem River, while Ruth avers he would rather do his hitting almost any place else. Their attitudes toward hitting in the stadium are reflected in the fact that the Babe has hit the majority of his home runs on the road, and Lou has made most of his at home.

New York Sun

Underneath second base in Yankee Stadium there once was a brick vault 15 feet wide that contained electrical, telephone, and miscellaneous equipment for boxing events.

baseball-almanac.com

FAST FACT: The vault was removed in 1976 during the major restoration of Yankee Stadium.

Yankee Stadium is the Rolls-Royce of stadiums.

Fernando Ferrer
former Bronx Borough president

———

The old stadium had a biblical look. I assumed it had been standing on 161st Street since before Christ. Years later, when I saw the actual Roman Colosseum, I couldn't suppress an inner gasp of recognition. Ahhh! It's like Yankee Stadium.

Laura Cunningham
author

———

The stadium was like the Empire State Building or the Grand Canyon of baseball, and every time I stepped inside of it, I had to pinch myself!

Mel Allen
19-year radio and television voice of the Yankees

There's the bigness of it. There are those high stands and all the people smoking and, of course, the shadows.

Ted Williams

Yankee Stadium was a mistake. Not mine, but the Giants.

Col. Jacob Ruppert
owner (1915–45)

People from out of town say there are three things in New York they want to see—the Statue of Liberty, Radio City, and Yankee Stadium. I guess you could say the stadium is hallowed ground.

Bill Waite
Yankee Stadium employee for more than 50 years

The filigreed gray-green facade above the third tier of the grandstand remains baseball's unscaled peak.

Donald Honig

It can be an intimidating thing your first few times there. All the lore of the stadium and the mystique can be difficult to deal with.

Al Leiter

The cathedral of baseball.

David Cone

It's the most magical park ever built. Playing there as a Yankee was like being in the Marines, the feeling that you were in a special ballpark, special town, special uniform, special history.

Phil Linz
infield (1962–65)

Being from New York, it meant a lot for me to play in my hometown. I knew every nook and cranny there, and we had the fans behind us. Back then, you had the monuments in the outfield and that was unbelievable.

Phil Rizzuto

Baseball heaven.

Randy Johnson
pitcher (2005–)

To play 18 years in Yankee Stadium is the best thing that could ever happen to a ballplayer.

Mickey Mantle

13

THE
RIVALRY

In order to have a Classic Rivalry, you have to have an ancient grievance. This one goes back to 1920, when Harry Frazee, who rates right up there in Boston's Hall of Infamy with King George III and tax stamps, sold Babe Ruth to the Yankees for $125,000.

Ed Linn
author

The dark age of Boston baseball can be traced directly to the sale of Babe Ruth to the Yankees. The golden age of Yankee baseball can be traced directly to their acquisition of the Bambino. The animosity, the ill feelings, the combative atmosphere that still characterize Red Sox-Yankee competition have much to do with the Frazee shuttle of players to New York.

Harvey Frommer

FAST FACT: While recent superstars like Wade Boggs, Roger Clemens, and Johnny Damon are the most prominently mentioned defections in the free agency era, the steady trail of quality players from Boston to New York, after the sale of Ruth, included Waite Hoyt, Herb Pennock, Red Ruffing, Joe Bush, Wally Schang, Everett Scott, Joe Dugan—all starters on Yankees world-championship teams.

I wish I'd never see them again. I wish they'd disappear from the league.

Pedro Martinez
former Boston Red Sox pitcher

We never talked to the opposing players the way they do now. In all the years I played against the Red Sox, I said hello to one person—Bobby Doerr—and all I said was Hello. I didn't want to.

Jerry Coleman

It's everything a rivalry ought to be. US AGAINST THEM. It's not only New York City against Boston. It's New York against New England. The canyons of Wall Street and the caverns of Madison Avenue vs. the White Hills of New Hampshire and the Green Mountains of Vermont.

Ed Linn

You have to play your best against them. It doesn't matter how bad they've been playing or how bad they've been struggling. You've got to bring your "A" game against them all the time.

David Ortiz

Boston Red Sox first baseman/ designated hitter

There's no comfort. We know what the Boston Red Sox are all about. We saw what they did last year. That's very clear in our minds.

Alex Rodriguez

on the insecurity of a slim one-game lead over the Red Sox heading into the final four games of the 2005 season, including the final three at Fenway. Boston's astounding comeback against New York in the 2004 ALCS paved the way for Boston's first World Series title since 1918

———

The Red Sox and the Yankees are two national teams. They are the greatest gate attractions everywhere. . . . It's the greatest rivalry in sports.

Haywood Sullivan

former Red Sox general partner and chief executive officer

There is no hype. You don't have to hype it up. You feel it. You walk into the clubhouse. You get into your car to drive to the ballpark. You get the paper in the morning. As a player you feel it. It singes you up a little bit.

Wade Boggs
third base (1993–97),
on the Boston-New York rivalry

———

Dent's homer, because Dent was a Yankee and losing a big game to the Yankees is the most terrible fate that can befall the Boston Red Sox on a ball field.

Tim McCarver
former St. Louis-Philadelphia
catcher/TV analyst,
asked what was the most
devastating play in Red Sox
history: Bucky Dent's homer
in '78 or Bill Buckner's blunder
against the Mets in '86

The division's best team, which also happens to be baseball's most expensive team, earned its latest East title by a margin as thin as a blade of Fenway infield grass. The perk? Even if Torre shows up at home plate Sunday in a pair of boxers and forfeits the game because his team popped one too many bottles of Korbel the night before, the Yankees still will own the division because of a better season record against The Nation.

Gene Wojciechowski

on the dramatic conclusion to the 2005 regular season at Boston

Throughout 1978, the entire Boston-New York series was handled like a playoff because of the history of bad blood between the teams.

Ron Luciano

former American League umpire

There was a traffic jam outside of Fenway as fans fought with each other trying to get home in time for *Hawaii Five-O.*

Anonymous Boston reporter

following the 15–3 Yankees annihilation of the Red Sox, Sept. 7, 1978—a rout that was 12–0 after four innings

⎯⎯⎯⎯⎯

There was a rivalry between the Sox and the Yankee fans, but Ted Williams rooted all the while for Joe DiMaggio to keep the streak going. As a hitter, Williams could appreciate the magnitude of the accomplishment. "You can talk all you want about Hornsby's .424 average," he said, "and Hack Wilson's 190 RBIs, but when DiMag hit in those 56 consecutive games, he put a line in the record book. It's one that will never be changed."

Harvey Frommer

When it came time for the 1941 Most Valuable Player award, it was Joe DiMaggio who was selected, not Ted Williams. . . . For Red Sox rooters, it was just a bit more salt on the wound in a rivalry that was not just New York-Boston but also Williams-DiMaggio.

Harvey Frommer

FAST FACT: Williams, in addition to hitting .406 that season—the last major-leaguer to hit .400—also led the American League in home runs, hits, walks, runs scored, and slugging percentage. While DiMaggio led the loop in RBIs, voters were most certainly swayed by "The Streak."

The way the Red Sox play is like the repeated sailing of the *Titanic*.

Thor Hansen
Yankees fan, New York City

Boston and New York fans are die-hard— hard on a player when he fails and right there to cheer when he succeeds.

Circo Tudisco
Brooklyn, N.Y.

14

THE SUBWAY
SERIES

*F*or almost as long as the Yankees have been play-ing baseball there has been a Subway Series—that interborough phenomenon that pits the Pinstripers against a National League champion also from New York City in the World Series.

There have been 14 of them, from the first Yankees-Giants clash in 1921 through the 2000 edi-tion versus the Mets. The Bronx Bombers have dom-inated the competition, taking 11 of the 14, includ-ing nine in a row from 1923 through '53.

The Giants played in the first five Subway Series, while the Brooklyn Dodgers faced the Yankees in seven of the next eight. The Mets are the third team to join the famous series and the most recent to taste defeat at the hands of New York's perennial champs.

1921

Spitballer "Shufflin'" Phil Douglas beats the Yankees twice in a thrilling best-of-nine series that sees Giants pitching hold the Yankees to a composite .207 batting average. Babe Ruth, who stunned fans and foes alike that year by recording a stupendous 59 regular-season home runs, is the only Yankee to hit over .300 for the series. The Yankees, behind Carl Mays and ace Waite Hoyt, shut out the Giants in the first two games, but John McGraw's scrappers claw back to take five of the next six. **Giants, 5–3.**

1922

Ruth, who goes just 2–for–17 (.118), is indicative of poor Yankees hitting in general (.203), as the Bombers fail to record a win in a five-game series against the Giants that produces an odd tie. Game two is called on account of darkness after 10 scoreless innings, and New Yorkers rifle the field with bottles and seat cushions in protest. Like the year before, with all games being played at the Polo Grounds, the Giants and Yankees alternate as home team. **Giants, 4–0–1.**

1923

The Yankees move into their new stadium across the Harlem River, the one that Ruth built. The fabulous stadium brings the Yanks a change in luck, as they gain their first world championship ever—over the New York Giants, their third Subway Series in successive years with John McGraw's men.

Ruth finally breaks out in this World Series, hitting three home runs and batting .368. A Giants outfielder named Casey Stengel helps the Giants to an opening-game win with his inside-the-park homer. **Yankees, 4–2**.

1936

After a 13-year hiatus, the Yanks and Giants resume their Subway feud. The Yankees unveil classy rookie Joe DiMaggio to go with sturdy veteran Lou Gehrig. Future immortal Lefty Gómez maintains his unbeaten World Series streak, collecting two series victories, as the Bombers overpower the Giants by scores of 18–4 and 13–5. The Clipper (nine hits) and star third baseman Red Rolfe, along with little-known outfielder Jake Powell, both with 10 hits apiece, pace the Yanks' barrage. **Yankees, 4–2**.

1937

In his final World Series as a Yankee, Tony "Poosh 'Em Up" Lazzeri hits .400 to aid an outstanding pitching effort by aces Lefty Gómez and Red Ruffing, who combine to beat the Giants on three complete-game wins. The Yanks, for the second year in a row and for the third straight time in a Subway Series, beat their National League city rivals. **Yankees, 4–1**.

1941

The year of Joe DiMaggio's unparalleled 56-game hitting streak winds up with the first Subway Series encounter against the Bums from Brooklyn. One of baseball's immortal moments occurs in Game Four, with the Dodgers holding a 4–3 edge in the top of the ninth. Dodgers reliever Hugh Casey strikes out Tommy Henrich for the apparent third out and a Brooklyn victory, but catcher Mickey Owen lets the strike-three pitch get away and Henrich reaches first. The Yanks rally for four runs, and the series turns. Instead of being even at two games apiece, it's 3–1 Yanks. They wrap up their ninth world title the next day. **Yankees, 4–1**.

1947

More memorable moments abound as the Yankees' Bill Bevens loses a Game Four no-hitter with two out in the bottom of the ninth, when Brooklyn pinch hitter Cookie Lavagetto doubles in two runs for a Dodgers victory to even the series. In Game Six, Joe DiMaggio is robbed by little substitute left fielder Joe Gionfriddo of a sure home run, preserving Brooklyn's series-tying win. Still, it's the Yanks who take the seventh and deciding game behind the shutout relief of Bevens and ace Joe Page. The first appearance of an African-American player in a World Series is made by the Dodgers' NL Rookie of the Year, Jackie Robinson. **Yankees, 4–3**.

1949

Again the Dodgers provide the Subway opposition as the Yankees begin their legendary run of five straight world championships. The Bombers hit just .226, but Brooklyn hits worse (.210). Allie "the Chief" Reynolds posts an ERA of 0.00 in 12.1 innings pitched as the Yanks rule in five games. **Yankees, 4–1**.

1951

This postseason is best remembered for a sub-Subway Series before the main event. In a one-game playoff, the Giants' Bobby Thomson hits "The Shot Heard 'Round the World," defeating Brooklyn to advance to the World Series opposite the Yanks.

The real Subway Series isn't nearly as memorable as the National League playoff, but it debuts a young pair of future superstars: the Giants' Willie Mays and the Yankees' Mickey Mantle. It is also the 10th and final World Series for an aging Joe DiMaggio, as well as the beginning of the injury-prone Mantle era. The rookie severely injures his knee in Game Two, playing right field, next to DiMaggio. **Yankees, 4–2.**

1952

The Dodgers take a 3–2 lead back to Ebbets Field, but clutch relief pitching from Allie Reynolds in games six and seven and critical home runs by Mantle in those two games bring the Bombers their 15th world championship. The play of the series is Billy Martin's flying, hats-off, last-second catch of Jackie Robinson's bases-loaded infield pop fly to preserve the Game Seven win. **Yankees, 4–3.**

1953

Billy Martin's heroics continue as the Yanks' second baseman hits .500, including two home runs, two triples, and eight runs batted in. Mickey Mantle contributes a pair of homers, and again Allie Reynolds is expert in relief, as the Bombers blitz Brooklyn. Martin's 12 hits, including the Game Six series-winner, ensures his selection as MVP. **Yankees, 4–2.**

1955

Salvation comes to Flatbush. The Dodgers finally embrace victory after seven humiliating attempts in World Series play. The Yankees' run of nine straight Subway Series triumphs ends as unlikely Brooklyn hero, pitcher Johnny Podres, twice beats the Bombers, including the finale in Game Seven. The series has some stellar moments, including Jackie Robinson's steal of home in the Bums' Game One loss, and Dodgers left fielder Sandy Amoros' foul-line robbery of a sure Yogi Berra opposite-field extra-base hit, with two runners on, to protect Podres's historic Game Seven win. **Brooklyn, 4–3.**

1956

Another seven-game thriller, a reverse carbon copy of the 1955 series. Every game was won by the team who had lost its equivalent the previous year. The Bombers took the decisive finale, 9–0, behind Johnny Kucks's three-hitter and Yogi Berra's pair of two-run homers. Icing it was Bill "Moose" Skowron's seventh-inning grand slam. The Yankees blast 12 homers in the series, including three each by Berra and Mantle. But the big slice of history is cut by an unassuming New York right-hander named Don Larsen, who in Game Five throws the one and only perfect game in World Series history. In that same game, Mantle's two-run homer and tremendous running catch of a deep left-center field fly in the fifth support Larsen's gem. **Yankees, 4–3**.

2000

It took 44 years for the Subway Series to surface once again, but thanks to the Yankees' 11th-hour awakening from a deadly late-season slumber and the Mets' matter-of-fact manhandling of the Giants and Cardinals, the talk turns to the No. 7 and No. 4 trains running those underground labyrinths under the streets of New York City.

It is worth the wait and the hype. The Yankees score 19 runs, the Mets 17. There is the 12-inning nail-biter that opens the Series and that some say takes the steam out of the Mets. A thrown splintered bat by Roger Clemens in the direction of Mike Piazza, inflaming an old wound that the press makes even more gaping, grabs almost as many headlines as the gem Clemens pitches in Game Two. A rising Yanks superstar at shortstop, Derek Jeter, in the end takes MVP honors for his omnipresent brilliance on the diamond, and lastly, there is of course talk of yet another Yankees dynasty— four world championships in five years.

The only thing token about the Yankees' 26 championships is the turnstile fare for this 14th Subway Series. **Yankees, 4–1.**

We are a part of history. We are something special. We were playing for more than the World Series. Now we have some bragging rights.

Bernie Williams

after the 2000 Subway Series, the 14th edition between the New York Yankees and New York's National League champion

The games were raw, emotional, edgy, a bit dangerous, bizarre, and ultimately tighter than a streetwalker's spandex.

Tom Verducci

Sports Illustrated, *Oct. 30, 2000, on the 2000 World Series between the Yankees and the Mets*

15

LIFE

Don't quit until every base is uphill.
Babe Ruth

There is no greater inspiration to any American boy than Lou Gehrig. For if this awkward, inept, and downright clumsy player that I knew in the beginning could through sheer drive and determination turn himself into the finest first-base-covering machine in all baseball, then nothing is impossible to any man or boy in the country.

Paul Gallico

I always believe that an honest question deserves an honest answer, but sometimes you get into trouble by saying the wrong thing.

Roger Maris

I prayed to my favorite, Saint Jude, as I had done all season. He is the patron saint for lost causes. . . . I had felt all along that Roger's chances of beating the record were nearly hopeless. I prayed the hardest that Roger would be protected from injuries. He had had so many. Above all, I have always prayed for what Roger and I believe in most—to do your level best no matter what you do.

Pat Maris

in the pregame hours, Oct. 1, 1961, the last game of the season, in which her husband hit his record-breaking 61st home run

The American people will always admire a man who overcomes great pressures to achieve an outstanding goal.

President John F. Kennedy

in a message to Roger Maris

Ever since I was a kid, I'd had the over-powering feeling that the breaks would never be mine. It was the first time I had come up with the right game in the right place.

Allie Reynolds

FAST FACT: Reynolds is the only Yankee to hurl two no-hitters (both in 1951). This quote refers to the opening game of the 1949 World Series—a nail-biting 1–0 thriller over the Brooklyn Dodgers that was not settled until Tommy Henrich's bottom-of-the-ninth home run. The victory was a turning point in Reynolds's career.

I admit that in the past I've been cautious about using rookies, but . . . sometimes, a young arm is better than an old head.

Miller Huggins
manager (1918–29)

A team is where a boy can prove his courage on his own. A gang is where a coward goes to hide.

Mickey Mantle

Baseball was my whole life. Nothing was ever as much fun as baseball.

Mickey Mantle

1988

I could never be a manager. I can't manage myself. What would I do with 25 other problems?

Mickey Mantle

My mom raised me to be independent. She taught me to speak my mind. She believed in me just like I am.

David Wells

⟞⟝

Scallions are the greatest cure for a batting slump ever invented.

Babe Ruth

⟞⟝

There is nothing so dead as a dead arm.

Benny Bengough
catcher (1923–30)

Now that I'm coming to the small end of the funnel, I find myself more and more reviewing my life and asking myself whether I'm justified in believing I was a success. I find myself in the quiet of night . . . thinking, "Could I have done this? Could I have done that? Would it have been commensurate with my character to do it?"

Waite Hoyt

If you saw that Yankees pitching too often, there would be a lot of guys doing different jobs.

Joe Rudi

16-year major-league outfielder

16

THE BRONX CLUBHOUSE

Some kids dream of joining the circus, others of becoming a major-league baseball player. As a member of the New York Yankees, I've gotten to do both.

Graig Nettles
on the Yankees' "Bronx Zoo"
days of the 1970s

You can call it the turning point in the history of the New York Yankees.

Ed Barrow
general manager (1921–45)

FAST FACT: With the Yankees dormant in next to last place in the American League, a $5,000 fine was levied against Babe Ruth for arriving late for a game in St. Louis in August 1925. Ruth had led a group of agitators on the club in defiance of manager Miller Huggins. Yankee management backed Huggins's fine—the largest ever imposed on a player in major-league baseball at the time. Soon the band of reprobates, Ruth included, began to fall in line and solidify as a powerhouse team.

I don't play cards, I don't play golf, and I don't go to the picture show. All that's left is baseball.

Casey Stengel

I married him for better or for worse, but not for lunch.

Hazel Weiss

wife of longtime Yankees general manager George Weiss, after experiencing her husband on a daily basis when he was forcibly retired from major-league baseball for a year (1960)

Outside of baseball, I think Casey loved dancing most.

Edna Stengel

IN 2005 . . .

- The Yankees became the first team in major-league history to hit 200 or more homers in six straight seasons.

- Yankees attendance went past 3 million for the seventh consecutive season.

- Aaron Small became the first Yankees pitcher to win his first nine decisions since Tommy John in 1979.

- The Yankees became the third major-league franchise to draw 4 million fans in a season, joining Toronto (1992 and '93) and Colorado (1993).

- Small became the first pitcher in Yankees history to begin his career in New York with 10 consecutive victories.

- Bernie Williams appeared in his record 120th postseason game.

- In a 7–3 loss to Minnesota on July 27, 2005, Hideki Matsui played in his 424th straight game, tying a major-league record for consecutive games played to start a career. Ernie Banks also played in 424 games, for the Chicago Cubs from 1953 to '56.

I was sitting here the other day, and I tried to remember what it was like to hit a home run and win a game. And I couldn't remember. It was like the whole thing happened to somebody else.

Mickey Mantle
on his fiftieth birthday

When I think of all those wasted hours, my God, what somebody with brains could have done with them. You could go to bed at three o'clock in the morning, because you wouldn't have to be out [at the park] until one o'clock. You could sleep until 11. All those wasted hours.

Mark Koenig

First place only counts on that last Sunday.

Joe Torre

on tight division races

In the 2005 postseason Alex Rodriguez pulled off a vanishing act worthy of Houdini, hitting .133 (2–for–15). Last year he had a 2–for–17 flop in the final four games of the AL Championship Series collapse against Boston.

Associated Press

I played great baseball all year, but I played like a dog the last five days. At the end of the day, you win or lose as a team, but I didn't show up. . . . I'm not going to hang my head. I'm going to learn from it and become a better Yankee.

Alex Rodriguez

on the conclusion of his 2005
AL MVP season

I've often thought that a lot of awards you get are made-up deals so you'll come to the dinners.

Mickey Mantle

1985

During my 18 years I came to bat almost 10,000 times. I struck out about 1,700 times and walked maybe 1,800 times. You figure a ballplayer will average about 500 at bats a season. That means I played seven years without ever hitting the ball.

Mickey Mantle

My uniform might have said Los Angeles, but in my heart, I was always a Yankee.

Bill "Moose" Skowron
first base (1954–62), following the Dodgers' 1963 four-game World Series sweep of New York, in which Skowron starred for L.A., batting .385 with one home run

George Is George. I mean that's what goes with the territory here. If you come on board here and don't understand how passionate the owner is, then you should go somewhere else.

Joe Torre
after his meeting with Steinbrenner in Tampa regarding his status as Yankee pilot for 2006

Oh, well, you weren't Mickey Mantle then!

Darrell Royal

legendary University of Texas football coach, upon meeting Mantle for what he thought was the first time

FAST FACT: Mantle corrected Royal, saying they had met before, when Mickey was being recruited by University of Oklahoma head coach Bud Wilkinson to play football for OU. Royal, the starting quarterback for the Sooners at the time, was given the task of showing the young Mantle around the campus.

—◈—

The more we lose, the more [George] Steinbrenner will fly in. And the more he flies, the better the chances of the plane crashing.

Graig Nettles

I realize I still want to do this thing. I still want to manage. There's only one place to manage in my estimation. It's been the best time I've ever had, these 10 years.

Joe Torre

*on his decision to return
to manage the Yankees for the
2006 season after meeting with
owner George Steinbrenner*

————

We didn't use the word love, but it was pretty warm. It was something more than cordial. I needed to hear that they want me to do what I do. I had to not only hear it, but hear the tone in which it was said.

Joe Torre

*on his meeting with boss
Steinbrenner that determined
his decision to continue with
the Yankees for 2006*

When I'm not hitting, my wife could pitch and get me out.

Roger Maris

If I'd just tried for them dinky singles, I could've batted around .600.

Babe Ruth

I always had good stuff, only some days it didn't work as well as others.

Allie Reynolds

Babe Ruth made a grave mistake when he gave up pitching. Working once a week, he might have lasted a long time and become a great star.

Tris Speaker

*22-year major-league Hall of Fame outfielder,
in the spring of 1921—the year Ruth clouted 59 home runs*

Owning the Yankees is like owning the Mona Lisa.

George Steinbrenner

⸺⸺

I've got a new invention. It's a revolving bowl for tired goldfish.

Lefty Gómez

⸺⸺

I never had a bad night in my life, but I've had a few bad mornings.

Lefty Gómez

⸺⸺

I was supposed to be a doctor. Then a priest. I took a little of each and played baseball.

Joe Torre

⸺⸺

From the manager to the coaches to every player in here, we have a clubhouse filled with MVPs.

Derek Jeter

Son, it ain't the water cooler that's striking you out.

> **Casey Stengel**
> *to a young Mickey Mantle,*
> *who, early in his career, would*
> *periodically vent his frustrations*
> *on the dugout water cooler,*
> *particularly after striking out.*

I hope he watches me and is pulling his hair out of his beard.

> **Orlando Hernández**
> *on Cuban dictator Fidel Castro*

He was my childhood.

> **Billy Crystal**
> *actor/comedian,*
> *at Mickey Mantle's funeral*

Babe Ruth's suitcase.

> **Ping Bodie**
> *outfield (1918–21),*
> *when asked who he roomed*
> *with when the Yankees were*
> *on the road*

I thank the Good Lord for making me a Yankee.

Joe DiMaggio

It's great to be young and a Yankee.

Waite Hoyt

There are those lucky ones of us who are able to say, "I was a Yankee."

Tommy Henrich

There are three things that are perfectly Yankee—the pinstripes, the logo, and Bob Sheppard's voice. When I go to heaven, I want Bob Sheppard to announce me.

Billy Crystal

17

WORLD CHAMPION ROSTERS

*T*he Yankees' extraordinary run of success has generated a luxurious bounty of gilded crowns. Twenty-six times the champions have sat on baseball's majestic throne, their record number of titles unequalled in the history of sport. Many a name in pinstripes has lent his talents to the almost mystical domain of Yankeedom. These players are the might behind the pennant flags, the winning laurels, the kingly crowns. They are the true lords of baseball.

THE 1923 YANKEES
98–54
Miller Huggins, manager

Benny Bengough,
catcher

Joe Bush, pitcher

Joe Dugan,
third base

Mike Gazella,
shortstop, second
and third base

Lou Gehrig,
first base

Hinkey Haines,
outfield

Harvey Hendrick,
outfield

Fred Hofmann,
catcher

Waite Hoyt, pitcher

Ernie Johnson,
shortstop
and third base

Sam Jones, pitcher

Mike McNally,
shortstop, second
and third base

Carl Mays, pitcher

Bob Meusel,
left field

Herb Pennock, pitcher

George Pipgras,
pitcher

Wally Pipp,
first base

Oscar Roettger,
pitcher

Babe Ruth,
right field
and first base

Wally Schang,
catcher

Everett Scott,
shortstop

Bob Shawkey, pitcher

Elmer Smith, outfield

Aaron Ward,
second base

Whitey Witt,
center field

THE 1927 YANKEES
110–44
Miller Huggins, manager

Benny Bengough,
catcher

Pat Collins,
catcher

Earle Combs,
center field

Joe Dugan,
third base

Cedric Durst,
outfield and first base

Mike Gazella,
third base
and shortstop

Lou Gehrig,
first base

Joe Giard, pitcher

Johnny Grabowski,
catcher

Waite Hoyt, pitcher

Mark Koenig,
shortstop

Tony Lazzeri,
second base

Bob Meusel,
left field

Wilcy Moore,
pitcher

Ray Morehart,
second base

Ben Paschal, outfield

Herb Pennock,
pitcher

George Pipgras,
pitcher

Dutch Ruether,
pitcher

Babe Ruth,
right field

Bob Shawkey.
pitcher

Urban Shocker,
pitcher

Myles Thomas,
pitcher

Julie Wera,
third base

THE 1928 YANKEES
101–53
Miller Huggins, manager

Benny Bengough, catcher

George Burns, first base

Archie Campbell, pitcher

Pat Collins, catcher

Earle Combs, center field

Stan Coveleski, pitcher

Bill Dickey, catcher

Joe Dugan, third base

Leo Durocher, shortstop and second base

Cedric Durst, outfield and first base

Mike Gazella, third base and shortstop

Lou Gehrig, first base

Johnny Grabowski, catcher

Fred Heimach, pitcher

Waite Hoyt, pitcher

Hank Johnson, pitcher

Mark Koenig, shortstop

Tony Lazzeri, second base

Bob Meusel, left field

Wilcy Moore, pitcher

Ben Paschal, outfield

Herb Pennock, pitcher

George Pipgras, pitcher

Gene Robertson, second and third base

Babe Ruth, right field

Rosy Ryan, pitcher

Al Shealy, pitcher

Myles Thomas, pitcher

Tom Zachary, pitcher

THE 1932 YANKEES
107–47
Joe McCarthy, manager

Johnny Allen, pitcher

Ivy Andrews, pitcher

Sammy Byrd, outfield

Jumbo Brown, pitcher

Ben Chapman,
left field

Earle Combs,
center field

Dusty Cooke,
pinch runner

Frankie Crosetti,
shortstop

Charlie Devens,
pitcher

Bill Dickey, catcher

Doc Farrell, infield

Lou Gehrig, first base

Joe Glenn, catcher

Lefty Gómez, pitcher

Myril Hoag, outfield
and first base

Hank Johnson, pitcher

Art Jorgens, catcher

Lyn Lary, infield
and outfield

Tony Lazzeri,
second base

Danny Macfayden,
pitcher

Wilcy Moore, pitcher

Johnny Murphy,
pitcher

Herb Pennock, pitcher

Eddie Phillips, catcher

George Pipgras,
pitcher

Gordon Rhodes,
pitcher

Red Ruffing, pitcher

Babe Ruth, right field

Jack Saltzgaver,
second base

Roy Schalk,
second base

Joe Sewell, third base

Ed Wells, pitcher

THE 1936 YANKEES
102–51
Joe McCarthy, manager

Johnny Broaca, pitcher

Jumbo Brown, pitcher

Ben Chapman, outfield

Frankie Crosetti, shortstop

Bill Dickey, catcher

Joe DiMaggio, center field

Lou Gehrig, first base

Joe Glenn, catcher

Lefty Gómez, pitcher

Bump Hadley, pitcher

Don Heffner, shortstop, second and third base

Myril Hoag, left field

Roy Johnson, outfield

Art Jorgens, catcher

Ted Kleinhans, pitcher

Tony Lazzeri, second base

Pat Malone, pitcher

Johnny Murphy, pitcher

Monte Pearson, pitcher

Jake Powell, outfield

Red Rolfe, third base

Red Ruffing, pitcher

Jack Saltzgaver, infield

Bob Seeds, outfield and third base

George Selkirk, right field

Steve Sundra, pitcher

Dixie Walker, outfield

Kemp Wicker, pitcher

THE 1937 YANKEES
102–52
Joe McCarthy, manager

Ivy Andrews, pitcher

Johnny Broaca, pitcher

Spud Chandler, pitcher

Frankie Crosetti, shortstop

Babe Dahlgren, pinch runner

Bill Dickey, catcher

Joe DiMaggio, center field

Lou Gehrig, first base

Joe Glenn, catcher

Lefty Gómez, pitcher

Bump Hadley, pitcher

Don Heffner, infield

Tommy Henrich, outfield

Myril Hoag, outfield

Roy Johnson, outfield

Art Jorgens, catcher

Tony Lazzeri, second base

Frank Makosky, pitcher

Pat Malone, pitcher

Johnny Murphy, pitcher

Monte Pearson, pitcher

Jake Powell, outfield

Red Rolfe, third base

Red Ruffing, pitcher

Jack Saltzgaver, first base

George Selkirk, outfield

Joe Vance, pitcher

Kemp Wicker, pitcher

THE 1938 YANKEES
99–53
Joe McCarthy, manager

Ivy Andrews,
pitcher

Joe Beggs, pitcher

Spud Chandler,
pitcher

Frankie Crosetti,
shortstop

Babe Dahlgren,
first and third base

Bill Dickey,
catcher

Joe DiMaggio,
center field

Atley Donald, pitcher

Wes Ferrell, pitcher

Lou Gehrig,
first base

Joe Glenn, catcher

Lefty Gómez, pitcher

Joe Gordon,
second base

Bump Hadley, pitcher

Tommy Henrich,
outfield

Myril Hoag, outfield

Art Jorgens,
catcher

Bill Knickerbocker,
second base
and shortstop

Johnny Murphy,
pitcher

Monte Pearson,
pitcher

Jake Powell,
outfield

Red Rolfe,
third base

Red Ruffing, pitcher

George Selkirk,
outfield

Lee Stine, pitcher

Steve Sundra, pitcher

Joe Vance, pitcher

THE 1939 YANKEES
106–45
Joe McCarthy, manager

Spud Chandler,
pitcher

Frankie Crosetti,
shortstop

Babe Dahlgren,
first base

Bill Dickey, catcher

Joe DiMaggio,
center field

Atley Donald, pitcher

Wes Ferrell, pitcher

Joe Gallagher,
outfield

Lou Gehrig,
first base

Lefty Gómez, pitcher

Joe Gordon,
second base

Bump Hadley, pitcher

Tommy Henrich,
outfield and first base

Oral Hildebrand,
pitcher

Art Jorgens, catcher

Charlie Keller,
left field

Bill Knickerbocker,
second base
and shortstop

Johnny Murphy,
pitcher

Monte Pearson,
pitcher

Jake Powell,
outfield

Red Rolfe,
third base

Buddy Rosar,
catcher

Red Ruffing, pitcher

Marius Russo,
pitcher

George Selkirk,
right field

Steve Sundra,
pitcher

THE 1941 YANKEES
101–53
Joe McCarthy, manager

Tiny Bonham,
pitcher

Frenchy Bordagaray,
outfield

Norm Branch, pitcher

Marv Breuer, pitcher

Spud Chandler,
pitcher

Frankie Crosetti,
shortstop
and third base

Bill Dickey, catcher

Joe DiMaggio,
center field

Atley Donald, pitcher

Lefty Gómez, pitcher

Joe Gordon,
second base

Tommy Henrich,
right field

Charlie Keller,
left field

Johnny Lindell,
pinch hitter

Johnny Murphy,
pitcher

Steve Peek, pitcher

Jerry Priddy, infield

Phil Rizzuto,
shortstop

Red Rolfe,
third base

Buddy Rosar, catcher

Red Ruffing, pitcher

Marius Russo, pitcher

George Selkirk,
outfield

Ken Silvestri, catcher

Charley Stanceu,
pitcher

Johnny Sturm,
first base

George Washburn,
pitcher

THE 1943 YANKEES
98–56
Joe McCarthy, manager

Tiny Bonham, pitcher

Hank Borowy, pitcher

Marv Breuer, pitcher

Tommy Byrne, pitcher

Spud Chandler, pitcher

Frankie Crosetti, shortstop

Bill Dickey, catcher

Atley Donald, pitcher

Nick Etten, first base

Joe Gordon, second base

Oscar Grimes, shortstop and first base

Rollie Hemsley, catcher

Billy Johnson, third base

Charlie Keller, outfield

Johnny Lindell, outfield

Bud Metheny, outfield

Johnny Murphy, pitcher

Aaron Robinson, pinch hitter

Marius Russo, pitcher

Ken Sears, catcher

Tuck Stainback, outfield

Snuffy Stirnweiss, shortstop and second base

Jim Turner, pitcher

Roy Weatherly, outfield

Butch Wensloff, pitcher

Bill Zuber, pitcher

THE 1947 YANKEES
97–57
Bucky Harris, manager

Yogi Berra,
catcher and outfield

Bill Bevens, pitcher

Bobby Brown,
third base, shortstop,
and outfield

Tommy Byrne, pitcher

Spud Chandler, pitcher

Allie Clark, outfield

Frank Colman, outfield

Frankie Crosetti, second
base and shortstop

Joe DiMaggio,
center field

Karl Drews, pitcher

Lonny Frey, second base

Randy Gumpert, pitcher

Tommy Henrich,
right field

Ralph Houk, catcher

Billy Johnson, third base

Don Johnson, pitcher

Charlie Keller, outfield

Johnny Lindell, left field

Sherm Lollar, catcher

Johnny Lucadello,
second base

Al Lyons, pitcher

George McQuinn,
first base

Bobo Newsom, pitcher

Joe Page, pitcher

Jack Phillips, first base

Mel Queen, pitcher

Vic Raschi, pitcher

Allie Reynolds, pitcher

Phil Rizzuto, shortstop

Aaron Robinson,
catcher

Ted Sepkowski,
pinch runner

Spec Shea, pitcher

Ken Silvestri, catcher

Dick Starr, pitcher

Snuffy Stirnweiss,
second base

Butch Wensloff, pitcher

Bill Wight, pitcher

THE 1949 YANKEES
97–57
Casey Stengel, manager

Hank Bauer, right field

Yogi Berra, catcher

Bobby Brown, third base

Ralph Buxton, pitcher

Tommy Byrne, pitcher

Hugh Casey, pitcher

Jerry Coleman, second base

Joe Collins, first base

Jim Delsing, outfield

Joe DiMaggio, outfield

Tommy Henrich, first base

Frank Hiller, pitcher

Ralph Houk, catcher

Billy Johnson, infield

Charlie Keller, outfield

Dick Kryhoski, first base

Johnny Lindell, outfield

Ed Lopat, pitcher

Cliff Mapes, center field

Cuddles Marshall, pitcher

Johnny Mize, first base

Fenton Mole, first base

Gus Niarhos, catcher

Joe Page, pitcher

Jack Phillips, first base

Duane Pillette, pitcher

Bob Porterfield, pitcher

Vic Raschi, pitcher

Allie Reynolds, pitcher

Phil Rizzuto, shortstop

Fred Sanford, pitcher

Spec Shea, pitcher

Charlie Silvera, catcher

Snuffy Stirnweiss, second and third base

Mickey Witek, pinch hitter

Gene Woodling, left field

THE 1950 YANKEES
98–56
Casey Stengel, manager

Hank Bauer, right field

Yogi Berra, catcher

Bobby Brown,
third base

Tommy Byrne, pitcher

Jerry Coleman,
second base

Joe Collins, first base

Jim Delsing, pinch hitter

Joe DiMaggio,
center field

Tom Ferrick, pitcher

Whitey Ford, pitcher

Tommy Henrich,
first base

Johnny Hopp,
first base and outfield

Ralph Houk, catcher

Jackie Jensen, outfield

Billy Johnson,
third base

Don Johnson, pitcher

Johnny Lindell, outfield

Ed Lopat, pitcher

Dave Madison, pitcher

Cliff Mapes, outfield

Billy Martin,
second and third base

Johnny Mize, first base

Ernie Nevel, pitcher

Joe Ostrowski, pitcher

Joe Page, pitcher

Bob Porterfield, pitcher

Vic Raschi, pitcher

Allie Reynolds, pitcher

Phil Rizzuto,
shortstop

Fred Sanford, pitcher

Charlie Silvera, catcher

Snuffy Stirnweiss,
second base

Dick Wakefield,
pinch hitter

Gene Woodling,
left field

Hank Workman,
first base

THE 1951 YANKEES
98–56
Casey Stengel, manager

Hank Bauer, right field

Yogi Berra, catcher

Jim Brideweser, shortstop

Bobby Brown, third base

Tommy Byrne, pitcher

Bob Cerv, outfield

Jerry Coleman, second base

Joe Collins, first base

Clint Courtney, catcher

Joe DiMaggio, center field

Tom Ferrick, pitcher

Johnny Hopp, first base

Ralph Houk, catcher

Jackie Jensen, outfield

Billy Johnson, third base

Jack Kramer, pitcher

Bob Kuzava, pitcher

Ed Lopat, pitcher

Gil McDougald, second and third base

Mickey Mantle, outfield

Cliff Mapes, outfield

Billy Martin, outfield, shortstop, second and third base

Johnny Mize, first base

Tom Morgan, pitcher

Ernie Nevel, pitcher

Joe Ostrowski, pitcher

Stubby Overmire, pitcher

Vic Raschi, pitcher

Allie Reynolds, pitcher

Phil Rizzuto, shortstop

Johnny Sain, pitcher

Fred Sanford, pitcher

Art Schallock, pitcher

Spec Shea, pitcher

Charlie Silvera, catcher

Bob Wiesler, pitcher

Archie Wilson, outfield

Gene Woodling, left field

THE 1952 YANKEES
95–59
Casey Stengel, manager

Loren Babe, third base
Hank Bauer, right field
Yogi Berra, catcher
Ewell Blackwell, pitcher
Jim Brideweser,
shortstop,
second and third base
Bobby Brown, third base
Andy Carey,
third base and shortstop
Bob Cerv, outfield
Jerry Coleman,
second base
Joe Collins, first base
Tom Gorman, pitcher
Bobby Hogue, pitcher
Johnny Hopp,
first base
Ralph Houk, catcher
Jackie Jensen, outfield
Charlie Keller, outfield
Bob Kuzava, pitcher
Ed Lopat, pitcher
Jim McDonald, pitcher

Gil McDougald,
third base
Mickey Mantle,
center field
Billy Martin, second base
Bill Miller, pitcher
Johnny Mize, first base
Tom Morgan, pitcher
Irv Noren, first base
and outfield
Joe Ostrowski, pitcher
Vic Raschi, pitcher
Allie Reynolds, pitcher
Phil Rizzuto, shortstop
Johnny Sain, pitcher
Ray Scarborough, pitcher
Harry Schaeffer, pitcher
Johnny Schmitz, pitcher
Kal Segrist,
second and third base
Charlie Silvera, catcher
Archie Wilson,
pinch hitter
Gene Woodling, left field

THE 1953 YANKEES
99–52
Casey Stengel, manager

Loren Babe, third base

Hank Bauer, right field

Yogi Berra, catcher

Ewell Blackwell, pitcher

Don Bollweg, first base

Jim Brideweser, shortstop

Andy Carey, second and third base and shortstop

Bob Cerv, pinch hitter

Jerry Coleman, second base and shortstop

Joe Collins, first base

Whitey Ford, pitcher

Tom Gorman, pitcher

Ralph Houk, catcher

Steve Kraly, pitcher

Bob Kuzava, pitcher

Ed Lopat, pitcher

Jim McDonald, pitcher

Gil McDougald, third base

Mickey Mantle, center field

Billy Martin, second base

Bill Miller, pitcher

Willy Miranda, shortstop

Johnny Mize, first base

Irv Noren, outfield

Vic Raschi, pitcher

Bill Renna, outfield

Allie Reynolds, pitcher

Phil Rizzuto, shortstop

Johnny Sain, pitcher

Ray Scarborough, pitcher

Art Schallock, pitcher

Art Schult, pinch runner

Charlie Silvera, catcher and third base

Gus Triandos, first base and catcher

Gene Woodling, right field

THE 1956 YANKEES
97–57
Casey Stengel, manager

Hank Bauer, right field

Yogi Berra, catcher

Tommy Byrne, pitcher

Andy Carey, third base

Tom Carroll, third base

Bob Cerv, outfield

Jerry Coleman, shortstop, second and third base

Rip Coleman, pitcher

Joe Collins, first base and outfield

Sonny Dixon, pitcher

Whitey Ford, pitcher

Bob Grim, pitcher

Elston Howard, left field

Billy Hunter, shortstop and third base

Jim Konstanty, pitcher

Johnny Kucks, pitcher

Don Larsen, pitcher

Jerry Lumpe, shortstop and third base

Mickey McDermott, pitcher

Mickey Mantle, center field

Billy Martin, second base

Gil McDougald, shortstop

Tom Morgan, pitcher

Irv Noren, outfield and first base

Bobby Richardson, second base

Phil Rizzuto, shortstop

Eddie Robinson, first base

Norm Siebern, outfield

Charlie Silvera, catcher

Lou Skizas, pinch hitter

Bill Skowron, first base

Enos Slaughter, outfield

Gerry Staley, pitcher

Tom Sturdivant, pitcher

Ralph Terry, pitcher

Bob Turley, pitcher

George Wilson, outfield

THE 1958 YANKEES
92–62
Casey Stengel, manager

Hank Bauer,
right field

Yogi Berra,
catcher and outfield

Andy Carey, third base

Bobby Delgreco,
outfield

Murry Dickson, pitcher

Art Ditmar, pitcher

Ryne Duren, pitcher

Whitey Ford, pitcher

Bob Grim, pitcher

Elston Howard,
catcher and outfield

Johnny James,
pitcher

Darrell Johnson, catcher

Tony Kubek, shortstop

Johnny Kucks, pitcher

Don Larsen, pitcher

Jerry Lumpe,
third base
and shortstop

Gil McDougald,
second base

Duke Maas, pitcher

Sal Maglie, pitcher

Mickey Mantle,
center field

Zach Monroe, pitcher

Bobby Richardson,
second and third base
and shortstop

Bobby Shantz, pitcher

Norm Siebern,
left field

Harry Simpson,
outfield

Bill Skowron,
first base

Enos Slaughter,
outfield

Tom Sturdivant,
pitcher

Marv Throneberry,
first base and outfield

Virgil Trucks, pitcher

Bob Turley, pitcher

THE 1961 YANKEES
109–53
Ralph Houk, manager

Luis Arroyo, pitcher

Yogi Berra, left field

Johnny Blanchard, catcher

Clete Boyer, third base

Bob Cerv, outfield

Tex Clevenger, pitcher

Jim Coates, pitcher

Bud Daley, pitcher

Joe Demaestri, shortstop

Art Ditmar, pitcher

Al Downing, pitcher

Whitey Ford, pitcher

Billy Gardner, third base

Jesse Gonder, pinch hitter

Bob Hale, first base

Elston Howard, catcher

Deron Johnson, third base

Tony Kubek, shortstop

Hector Lopez, outfield

Danny McDevitt, pitcher

Mickey Mantle, center field

Roger Maris, right field

Jack Reed, outfield

Hal Reniff, pitcher

Bobby Richardson, second base

Rollie Sheldon, pitcher

Bill Skowron, first base

Bill Stafford, pitcher

Ralph Terry, pitcher

Lee Thomas, pinch hitter

Earl Torgeson, first base

Tom Tresh, shortstop

Bob Turley, pitcher

THE 1962 YANKEES
96–66
Ralph Houk, manager

Luis Arroyo, pitcher

Johnny Blanchard,
outfield and catcher

Yogi Berra, catcher

Jim Bouton, pitcher

Clete Boyer,
third base

Marshall Bridges,
pitcher

Hal Brown, pitcher

Bob Cerv, outfield

Tex Clevenger,
pitcher

Jim Coates, pitcher

Bud Daley, pitcher

Whitey Ford,
pitcher

Billy Gardner,
second and third base

Jake Gibbs, third base

Elston Howard,
catcher

Tony Kubek,
shortstop and outfield

Phil Linz, shortstop

Dale Long, first base

Hector Lopez,
left field

Mickey Mantle,
center field

Roger Maris,
right field

Joe Pepitone,
outfield

Jack Reed, outfield

Bobby Richardson,
second base

Rollie Sheldon, pitcher

Bill Skowron,
first base

Bill Stafford, pitcher

Ralph Terry, pitcher

Tom Tresh, shortstop

Bob Turley, pitcher

THE 1977 YANKEES
100–62
Billy Martin, manager

Dell Alston, outfield

Dave Bergman, outfield

Paul Blair, outfield

Chris Chambliss,
first base

Ken Clay, pitcher

Bucky Dent, shortstop

Dock Ellis, pitcher

Ed Figueroa, pitcher

Ron Guidry, pitcher

Don Gullett, pitcher

Fran Healy, catcher

Ellie Hendricks, catcher

Ken Holtzman, pitcher

Catfish Hunter, pitcher

Reggie Jackson,
right field

Cliff Johnson, catcher

Dave Kingman,
designated hitter

Mickey Klutts,
third base

Gene Locklear, outfield

Sparky Lyle, pitcher

Larry McCall, pitcher

Carlos May, outfield

Thurman Munson,
catcher

Graig Nettles,
third base

Gil Patterson, pitcher

Marty Perez,
third base

Lou Piniella,
designated hitter

Willie Randolph,
second base

Mickey Rivers,
center field

Fred Stanley, shortstop

Stan Thomas, pitcher

Dick Tidrow, pitcher

Mike Torrez, pitcher

Roy White, left field

Jim Wynn, outfield

George Zeber,
second base

THE 1978 YANKEES
100–63
Billy Martin, Dick Howser, and **Bob Lemon,**
managers

Dell Alston, pinch hitter

Jim Beattie, pitcher

Paul Blair, outfield

Chris Chambliss,
first base

Ken Clay, pitcher

Bucky Dent, shortstop

Brian Doyle, second base

Rawly Eastwick, pitcher

Ed Figueroa, pitcher

Damaso Garcia,
second base

Rich Gossage, pitcher

Ron Guidry, pitcher

Don Gullett, pitcher

Fran Healy, catcher

Mike Heath, catcher

Ken Holtzman, pitcher

Catfish Hunter, pitcher

Reggie Jackson,
right field

Cliff Johnson,
designated hitter

Jay Johnstone, outfield

Bob Kammeyer, pitcher

Mickey Klutts, third base

Paul Lindblad, pitcher

Sparky Lyle, pitcher

Larry McCall, pitcher

Andy Messersmith,
pitcher

Thurman Munson,
catcher

Graig Nettles, third base

Lou Piniella, outfield

Willie Randolph,
second base

Mickey Rivers,
center field

Dennis Sherrill, third base

Jim Spencer,
designated hitter

Fred Stanley, shortstop

Gary Thomasson, outfield

Dick Tidrow, pitcher

Roy White,
designated hitter

George Zeber,
second base

THE 1996 YANKEES
92–70
Joe Torre, manager

Mike Aldrete, outfield

Wade Boggs, third base

David Cone, pitcher

Mariano Duncan, second base

Robert Eenhoorn, first base

Cecil Fielder, designated hitter

Andy Fox, second base

Joe Girardi, catcher

Dwight Gooden, pitcher

Charlie Hayes, third base

Matt Howard, second base

Dion James, outfield

Derek Jeter, shortstop

Pat Kelly, second base

Jimmy Key, pitcher

Jim Leyritz, catcher

Matt Luke, designated hitter

Tim McIntosh, catcher

Tino Martinez, first base

Ramiro Mendoza, pitcher

Jeff Nelson, pitcher

Paul O'Neill, right field

Andy Pettitte, pitcher

Jorge Posada, catcher

Tim Raines, outfield

Mariano Rivera, pitcher

Ruben Rivera, outfield

Kenny Rogers, pitcher

Ruben Sierra, designated hitter

Luis Sojo, second base

Darryl Strawberry, outfield

John Wetteland, pitcher

Bob Wickman, pitcher

Bernie Williams, center field

Gerald Williams, left field

THE 1998 YANKEES
114–48
Joe Torre, manager

Scott Brosius,
third base

Homer Bush,
second base

David Cone, pitcher

Chad Curtis,
left field

Chili Davis,
designated hitter

Mike Figga, catcher

Joe Girardi, catcher

Orlando Hernández,
pitcher

Hideki Irabu, pitcher

Derek Jeter,
shortstop

Chuck Knoblauch,
second base

Ricky Ledee, outfield

Mike Lowell,
third base

Tino Martinez,
first base

Ramiro Mendoza,
pitcher

Jeff Nelson, pitcher

Paul O'Neill,
right field

Andy Pettitte,
pitcher

Jorge Posada,
catcher

Tim Raines, outfield

Luis Sojo, infield

Shane Spencer,
outfield

Mike Stanton,
pitcher

Darryl Strawberry,
outfield

Dale Sveum,
first base

David Wells, pitcher

Bernie Williams,
center field

THE 1999 YANKEES
98–64
Joe Torre, manager

Clay Bellinger,
infield and outfield

Scott Brosius,
third base

Roger Clemens,
pitcher

David Cone, pitcher

Chad Curtis,
left field

Chili Davis,
designated hitter

Joe Girardi, catcher

Orlando Hernández,
pitcher

Hideki Irabu, pitcher

Derek Jeter,
shortstop

D'Angelo Jimenez,
third base

Chuck Knoblauch,
second base

Ricky Ledee,
outfield

Jim Leyritz, catcher

Jeff Manto,
third base

Tino Martinez,
first base

Paul O'Neill,
right field

Andy Pettitte,
pitcher

Jorge Posada,
catcher

Luis Sojo, infield

Alfonso Soriano,
shortstop

Shane Spencer,
outfield

Mike Stanton, pitcher

Darryl Strawberry,
outfield

Tony Tarasco,
outfield

Bernie Williams,
center field

THE 2000 YANKEES
87–74
Joe Torre, manager

Clay Bellinger, outfield

Scott Brosius, third base

Jose Canseco, outfield

Roger Clemens, pitcher

David Cone, pitcher

Wilson Delgado, second base

Todd Erdos, pitcher

Dwight Gooden, pitcher

Jason Grimsley, pitcher

Orlando Hernández, pitcher

Glenallen Hill, outfield

Derek Jeter, shortstop

Lance Johnson, outfield

Felix Jose, outfield

David Justice, outfield

Roberto Kelly, outfield

Chuck Knoblauch, second base

Ricky Ledee, outfield

Jim Leyritz, catcher

Tino Martinez, first base

Jeff Nelson, pitcher

Paul O'Neill, right field

Andy Pettitte, pitcher

Luis Polonia, outfield

Jorge Posada, catcher

Luis Sojo, infield

Alfonso Soriano, shortstop

Shane Spencer, outfield

Mike Stanton, pitcher

Ryan Thompson, outfield

Chris Turner, catcher

Jose Vizcaino, infield

Bernie Williams, center field

YANKEES IN THE
HALL OF FAME

(Year of induction in parentheses)

Ed Barrow (1953)

Yogi Berra (1970)

Jack Chesbro (1946)

Earle Combs (1970)

Bill Dickey (1954)

Joe DiMaggio (1955)

Whitey Ford (1974)

Lou Gehrig (1939)

Lefty Gómez (1972)

Waite Hoyt (1969)

Miller Huggins (1964)

Jim "Catfish" Hunter (1987)

Reggie Jackson (1993)

Willie Keeler (1939)

Tony Lazzeri (1991)

Joe McCarthy (1957)

Larry MacPhail (1978)

Lee MacPhail (1998)

Mickey Mantle (1974)

Herb Pennock (1948)

Phil Rizzuto (1994)

Red Ruffing (1967)

Babe Ruth (1936)

Casey Stengel (1966)

George Weiss (1970)

BIBLIOGRAPHY

Allen, Maury. *You Could Look It Up: The Life of Casey Stengel*. New York: Times Books, 1979.

Anderson, Dave et al. *The Yankees: The Four Fabulous Eras of Baseball's Most Famous Team*. New York: Random House, 1979.

Auchincloss, Kenneth. "Play Ball." *Newsweek*, Oct. 30, 2000, 63.

Beach, Jerry. *Godzilla Takes the Bronx: The Inside Story of Hideki Matsui*. Lanham, Md.: Taylor Trade Publishing, 2004.

Berra, Yogi. *The Yogi Book: "I Really Didn't Say Everything I Said!"* New York: Workman Publishing, 1998.

Blatt, Howard. *This Championship Season*. New York: Simon & Schuster, 1998.

Dame, Kevin T. *Yankee Stadium in Your Pocket*. Charlottesville, Va.: Baseball Direct, 1999.

David, Jay. *The New York Yankees: Legendary Heroes, Magical Moments, and Amazing Stats Through the Decades*. New York: Morrow and Co., 1997.

Frommer, Harvey. *A Yankee Century*. New York: The Berkley Publishing Group, 2002.

Frommer, Harvey. *Baseball's Greatest Rivalry*. New York: Atheneum, 1982.

Hageman, William, and Warren Wilbert. *New York Yankees: Seasons of Glory*. Middle Village, N.Y.: Jonathan David Publishers, 1999.

Halberstam, David. *Summer of '49*. New York: Morrow and Co., 1989.

Henrich, Tommy with Bill Gilbert. *Five O'Clock Lightning: Ruth, Gehrig, DiMaggio, Mantle and the Glory Years of the NY Yankees*. New York: Carol Publishing Group, 1992.

Herskowitz. Mickey. *Mickey Mantle: An Appreciation*. New York: Morrow and Co., 1995.

Honig, Donald. *Classic Baseball Photographs, 1869–1947*. New York: Smithmark, 1999.

———. *Mays, Mantle, Snider: A Celebration*. New York: Macmillan, 1987.

Kahn, Roger. *October Men: Reggie Jackson, George Steinbrenner, Billy Martin, and the Yankees' Miraculous Finish in 1978*. Orlando, Fla.: Harcourt, Inc., 2003.

Lally, Richard. *Bombers: An Oral History of the New York Yankees*. New York: Crown Publishers, 2002.

Linn, Ed. *The Great Rivalry: The Yankees and the Red Sox, 1901–1990*. NewYork: Ticknor & Fields, 1991.

Mantle, Mickey, and Phil Pepe. *Mickey Mantle: My Favorite Summer, 1956*. New York: Doubleday, 1991.

Mosedale, John. *The Greatest of All: The 1927 New York Yankees*. New York: Dial Press, 1974.

Pepe, Phil. *The Yankees: An Authorized History of the New York Yankees*. 3d Edition. Dallas, Tex.: Taylor, 1998.

Peyer, Tom, and Hart Seely, ed. *O Holy Cow! The Selected Verse of Phil Rizzuto*. Hopewell, N.J.: Ecco Press, 1993.

Robinson, Ray, and Christopher Jennison. *Yankee Stadium: 75 Years of Drama, Glamor, and Glory*. New York: Penguin Studio, 1998.

Rosenfeld, Harvey. *Roger Maris: A Title to Fame*. Fargo, N.D.: Prairie House, 1991.

Ruth, George Herman. *Babe Ruth's Own Book of Baseball*. New York: Putnam, 1928.

Saraceno, Jon. "Yankees Show How Pros Do Job." *USA Today*, Oct. 27, 2000, 3C.

Stout, Glenn and Richard A. Johnson. *Yankees Century: 100 Years of New York Yankees Baseball*. Boston, Mass.: Houghton Mifflin Company, 2002.

Thorn, John et al. *Total Baseball: The Official Encyclopedia of Major League Baseball*, Fifth Edition. New York: Viking Penguin, 1997.

Tullius, John. *I'd Rather Be a Yankee*. New York: Macmillan, 1986.

Vanderberg, Bob. *Minnie and the Mick*. South Bend, Ind.: Diamond Communications, 1996.

Verducci, Tom. "Roger & Out" *Sports Illustrated*, Oct. 30, 2000, 42.

Wheeler, Lonnie. *The Official Baseball Hall of Fame Story of Mickey Mantle*. New York: Simon & Schuster, 1990.

WEB SITES

AskMen.com. "Men of the Week: Businessmen — George Steinbrenner." http://www.askmen.com/men/business_politics/31c_george_steinbrenner.html.

Associated Press. "Shortstop follows in footsteps of Ruth, Gehrig." http://espn.go.com/mlb/news/2003/0603/1562514.html, June 5, 2003.

Associated press. "Yankees over .500 for first time since April 9." http://sports.espn.go.com/mlb/recap?gameId=250516112, May 16, 2005.

Associated Press. "Big Unit pounded for seven runs in three innings."
http://sports.espn.go.com/mlb/recap?gameId=250621110, June 21, 2005.

Associated Press. "Giambi and Martinez send balls sailing over fence twice."
http://sports.espn.go.com/mlb/recap?gameId=250720113, July 20, 2005.

Associated Press. "Small wins second straight start for Yankees."
http://sports.espn.go.com/mlb/recap?gameId=250728110, July 28, 2005.

Associated Press. "Giambi hits two homers, reaches 300 for career."
http://sports.espn.go.com/mlb/recap?gameId=250731110, July 31, 2005.

Associated Press. "Rivera records career-best 30th consecutive save."
http://sports.espn.go.com/mlb/recap?gameId=250808110, Aug. 8, 2005.

Associated Press. "Matsui homer sends Rangers to seventh straight loss."
http://sports.espn.go.com/mlb/recap?gameId=250814110, Aug. 14, 2005.

Associated Press. "Affeldt miscue sparks Yankees' winning rally."
http://sports.espn.go.com/mlb/recap?gameId=250827110, Aug. 27, 2005

Associated Press. "Pitching, defense abandon Red Sox in Bronx."
http://sports.espn.go.com/mlb/recap?gameId=250909110, Sept. 9, 2005.

Associated Press. "Blue Jays score seven late runs but can't tie game."
http://sports.espn.go.com/mlb/recap?gameId=250916114, Sept. 16, 2005.

Associated Press. "Mussina returns with four hitter, Yanks edge O's 7–6, 1? up."
http://sports.espn.go.com/mlb/recap?gameId=250922110, Sept. 22, 2005.

Associated Press. "Small wins 9th, remains unbeaten."
http://sports.espn.go.com/mlb/recap?gameId=250920110, Sept. 20, 2005.

Associated Press. "Yanks regain first place, beat Os 2–1."
http://sports.espn.go.com/mlb/recap?gameId=250921110, Sept. 21, 2005.

Associated Press. "Jeter, Robinson back-to-back leadoff HRs pace Yanks win over Jays, still game up."
http://sports.espn.go.com/mlb/recap?gameId=250923110, Sept. 23, 2005.

Associated Press. "Jared Wright blasted by hit ball for third time as Yanks lose. Tied with Bosox."
http://sports.espn.go.com/mlb/recap?gameId=250924110, Sept. 24, 2005.

Associated Press. "Adios Bernie, as longball gives Yankees 8–4 win over Jays."
http://sports.espn.go.com/mlb/recap?gameId=250925110, Sept. 25, 2005.

Associated Press. "Final Week-Yanks shell Baltimore 11–3, up lead over Bosox."
http://sports.espn.go.com/mlb/recap?gameId=250926101, Sept. 26, 2005.

Associated Press. "Chacon, Rodriguez propel Yanks to full game lead, four left."
http://sports.espn.go.com/mlb/recap?gameId=250928101, Sept. 28, 2005.

Associated Press. "Small wins 10th, Yanks stay in 1st, head to Boston."
http://newyork.yankees.mlb.com/NASApp/mlb/news/gameday_recap.jsp?ymd
=20050929&content_id=1230107&vkey=recap&fext=.jsp&c_id=nyy, Sept. 29, 2005.

Associated Press. "Angels let Yanks slip away — ALDS tied 2–2."
http://sports.espn.go.com/mlb/recap?gameId=251009110, Oct. 9, 2005.

Associated Press. "Colon leaves early, but Angels 'pen shuts down Yanks."
http://sports.espn.go.com/mlb/recap?gameId=251010103, Oct. 10, 2005.

Associated Press. "Bombers: $203M bust: Boss chides team, vows to 'do better'"
http://www.recordonline.com/archive/2005/10/12/mlbc12.htm, Oct. 12, 2005.

Associated Press. "Torre to return as Yanks manager in 2006."
http://www.usatoday.com/sports/baseball/al/yankees/2005-10-18-torre-return-ing_x.htm, Oct. 18, 2005.

Associated Press. "A-Rod's first-place votes outnumber Ortiz's by five."
http://sports.espn.go.com/mlb/news/story?id=2223736, Nov. 14, 2005.

baseball-almanac.com. "Graig Nettles."
http://www.baseball-almanac.com/players/player.php?p=nettlgr01.

baseball-almanac.com. "Quotations about the New York Yankees Franchise."
http://www.baseball-almanac.com/teams/yankquot.shtml.

baseball-almanac.com. "Quotations From & About Lou Gehrig."
http://www.baseball-almanac.com/quotes/quogehr.shtml.

baseball-almanac.com. "Yankee Stadium."
http://www.baseball-almanac.com/stadium/yankee_stadium.shtml.

baseball-reference.com.

Caple, Jim. "Potential bitter ending for Williams." ESPN.com.
http://sports.espn.go.com/mlb/playoffs2005/columns/story?columnist=caple
_jim&id=2187067, Oct. 10, 2005.

ESPN.com news services. "Yankees, Farnsworth agree to 3-year, $17M contract."
http://sports.espn.go.com/mlb/news/story?id=2245182, Dec. 2, 2005.

Feinsand, Mark. "Yankees rally late to defeat Angels: Bombers take lead in
seventh inning, force Game 5." mlb.com.
http://newyork.yankees.mlb.com/NASApp/mlb/news/gameday_recap.jsp?ymd=
20051009&content_id=1244183&vkey=recap&fext=.jsp&c_id=nyy, Oct. 9, 2005.

Feinsand, Mark. "Rodriguez's struggles mark ALDS loss: Third baseman posts
.133 average over five-game set." mlb.com.
http://newyork.yankees.mlb.com/NASApp/mlb/news/article.jsp?ymd=200510
11&content_id=1245761&vkey=news_nyy&fext=.jsp&c_id=nyy, Oct. 11, 2005.

Feinsand, Mark. "Steinbrenner thanks the fans: Owner compliments Angels,
promises Yanks 'will do better.'" mlb.com.
http://newyork.yankees.mlb.com/NASApp/mlb/news/article.jsp?ymd=200510
11&content_id=1246704&vkey=news_nyy&fext=.jsp&c_id=nyy, Oct. 11, 2005.

Neel, Eric. "Greatest Pitching Feats: Best of Last 25 Years" Page Two, ESPN.com.
http://sports.espn.go.com, Sept. 16, 2005.

newyork.yankees.mlb.com. "History: Yankees Owners."
http://newyork.yankees.mlb.com/NASApp/mlb/nyy/history/owners.jsp.

Rovell, Darren. "Arena named Jimmy Fund Center instead." ESPN.com.
http://sports.espn.go.com/mlb/news/story?id=1999921, Feb. 25, 2005

Urban, Mychael. "Rivera closes door on Angels . . ." newyork.yankees. mlb.com.
http://newyork.yankees.mlb.com/NASApp/mlb/news/article.jsp?ymd=200510
09&content_id=1244200&vkey=news_nyy&fext=.jsp&c_id=nyy, Oct. 9, 2005.

Urban, Mychael. "Yanks' defensive woes contribute to loss: Crosby, Sheffield
collision one of many miscues in ALDS."MLB.com.
http://newyork.yankees.mlb.com/NASApp/mlb/news/article.jsp?ymd=200510
10&content_id=1245253&vkey=news_nyy&fext=.jsp&c_id=nyy, Oct. 11, 2005.

USA TODAY.com: "George Is George" audio clip, Oct. 18, 2005.

Wojciechowski, Gene. "Dead even with two to play . . ." ESPN.com.
http://sports.espn.go.com/espn/columns/story?columnist=wojciechowski_gene
&id=2177605, Oct. 1, 2005.

Wojciechowski, Gene. "Yankees' winning formula: Hard work, team work."
ESPN.com.
http://sports.espn.go.com/espn/columns/story?columnist=wojciechowski_gene
&id=2178200, Oct. 3, 2005.

INDEX

A
Aaron, Henry, 114
Adams, Franklin P., 73
Aldrete, Mike, 242
Allen, Johnny, 223
Allen, Maury, 34, 83
Allen, Mel, 175
All-Star Game, 44, 161
Alston, Dell, 240-241
American League, 22, 28, 50, 57, 84, 89-90, 96, 106, 118, 123, 136-137, 141-142, 145, 154, 158-159, 167, 171, 177, 184, 186, 206, 210, 222, 230, 238
AL Championship Series (ALCS), 137, 182, 210
AL Divisional Series (ALDS), 143-144
AL East Division, 50, 118, 141-142
Amoros, Sandy, 193
Anderson, Dave, 15
Andrews, Ivy, 223, 225-226
Arizona Diamondbacks, 41
Arroyo, Luis, 238-239
Associated Press, 50, 141, 210
Atlanta Braves, 42, 102, 126, 163
Auchincloss, Kenneth, 25

B
Babe, Loren, 234-235
Baltimore Orioles, 50, 91, 96, 137, 142
Banks, Ernie, 208
Barrow, Ed, 74, 206, 246
Bauer, Hank, 11-12, 34, 231-237
Beattie, Jim, 241
Beggs, Joe, 226

Bellinger, Clay, 244-245
Bench, Johnny, 81
Bengough, Benny, 202, 220-222
Bergman, Dave, 240
Berra, Lawrence Peter "Yogi," 9, 12, 27, 53-54, 56, 58, 60, 80-81, 82, 83, 116, 120, 162, 168, 193-194, 230-239, 246
Bevens, Bill, 191, 230
Big Red Machine, 151
Black Sox Scandal, 67
Blackwell, Ewell, 234-235
Blair, Paul, 38, 240-241
Blanchard, Johnny, 238-239
Bodie, Ping, 217
Boggs, Wade, 180, 183, 242
Bollweg, Don, 235
Bonds, Barry, 96
Bonham, Tiny, 228-229
Bordagaray, Frenchy, 228
Borowy, Hank, 229
Boston Braves, 83-84
Boston Red Sox, 47, 49-50, 87, 96, 116, 118, 132, 136, 142, 156, 163, 179-186, 210
Bouton, Jim, 239
Boyer, Clete, 36, 238-239
Branch, Norm, 228
Brett, George, 150
Breuer, Marv, 228-229
Brideweser, Jim, 233-235
Bridges, Marshall, 239
Briggs Stadium, 106
Broaca, Johnny, 224-225
Brock, Lou, 113
Bronx Zoo, 205
Brooklyn Dodgers, 13, 55, 57, 59, 80, 128, 186-187, 190-193, 200

Brosius, Scott, 243-245
Broun, Heywood, 67
Brown, Bobby, 230-234
Brown, Hal, 239
Brown, Jumbo, 223-224
Buckner, Bill, 183
Burns, George, 222
Bush, Homer, 243
Bush, Joe, 180, 220
Buxton, Ralph, 231
Byrd, Sammy, 223
Byrne, Tommy, 229-233, 236

C
Cadore, Leon, 55
Campbell, Archie, 222
Cannon, Jimmy, 164
Cano, Robinson, 42, 98, 141
Canseco, Jose, 245
Carey, Andy, 27, 234-237
Carmichael, John, 127
Carroll, Tom, 236
Casey, Hugh, 190, 231
Castro, Fidel, 217
Cerv, Bob, 27, 233-236, 238-239
Chacon, Shawn, 40, 51, 98, 102, 143
Chambliss, Chris, 240-241
Chandler, Spud, 27, 225-230
Chapman, Ben, 223-224
Chesbro, Jack, 123, 246
Chicago Cubs, 22, 126-127, 208
Chicago White Sox, 41, 49, 84, 106
Cincinnati Reds, 13, 22, 54, 96, 126, 149, 151
Clark, Allie, 27, 230

Clay, Ken, 240-241
Clemens, Roger, 21, 52, 120, 180, 195, 244-245
Cleveland Indians, 18, 34, 84, 119, 124, 152
Clevenger, Tex, 238-239
Coates, Jim, 238-239
Cobb, Ty, 47, 66, 74, 78, 163
Cochrane, Mickey, 79
Coleman, Jerry, 112, 162, 181, 231-236
Coleman, Rip, 236
Collins, Joe, 231-236
Collins, Pat, 221-222
Colman, Frank, 230
Colorado Rockies, 208
Combs, Earle, 17, 32, 221-223, 246
Comiskey Park, 106
Cone, David, 37, 47, 123, 138, 177, 242-245
Connelly, Timmy, 159
Cooke, Dusty, 223
Cooper, Gary, 21
Courtney, Clint, 233
Coveleski, Stan, 222
Creamer, Robert W., 83, 107
Crosby, Bubba, 144
Crosetti, Frank "Frankie," 113, 223-230
Crystal, Billy, 11, 22, 217-218
Cunningham, Laura, 175
Curtis, Chad, 243-244
Cy Young Award, 166

D
Dahlgren, Babe, 225-227
Daley, Arthur, 127
Daley, Bud, 238-239
Damon, Johnny, 21, 180
Daniel, Dan, 148, 170
David, Jay, 70, 78, 151
Davis, Chili, 17, 243-244
Delgado, Wilson, 245
Delgreco, Bobby, 237
Delsing, Jim, 231-232
Demaestri, Joe, 238
Dent, Bucky, 117, 123, 136, 240-241
Detroit Tigers, 22, 28, 79, 96, 106, 110
Devens, Charlie, 223
Dickey, Bill, 12, 27, 60, 74, 222-229, 246

Dickson, Murry, 237
DiMaggio, Joe, "Joltin' Joe," "the Yankee Clipper," 3, 9, 12, 23, 25, 27, 32, 38, 42, 45, 54, 74-75, 76, 77-79, 116, 120, 142, 148, 154, 157, 164, 168, 185-186, 189-192, 218, 224-228, 230-233, 246
Ditmar, Art, 237-238
Dixon, Sonny, 236
Doerr, Bobby, 181
Donald, Atley, 226-229
Douglas, "Shufflin'" Phil, 188
Downing, Al, 238
Doyle, Brian, 241
Drews, Karl, 230
Dugan, "Jumpin'" Joe, 33-34, 66, 147, 180, 220-222
Duncan, Mariano, 242
Duren, Ryne, 237
Durocher, Leo, 222
Durst, Cedric, 221-222

E
Eastwick, Rawly, 241
Ebbets Field, 55, 192
Eenhoorn, Robert, 242
Ellis, Dock, 240
Erdos, Todd, 245
Erskine, Carl, 59
ESPN, 99, 102, 116, 118
Etten, Nick, 229

F
Fain, Ferris, 12
Farnsworth, Kyle, 42
Farrell, Doc, 223
Feller, Bob, 34
Fenway Park, 118, 136, 141, 182, 184-185
Ferrell, Wes, 226-227
Ferrer, Fernando, 175
Ferrick, Tom, 232-233
Fielder, Cecil, 242
Figga, Mike, 243
Figueroa, Ed, 240-241
Fischer, Bill, 135
FleetCenter, 116-117
Ford, Whitey, 12, 20, 27, 35, 86, 134, 166, 168, 232, 235-239, 246
Fothergill, Bob "Fatty," 28
Fox, Andy, 242

Foxx, Jimmie, 96
Frank, Stanley, 23
Frazee, Harry, 179-180
Frey, Lonny, 230
Frick, Ford, 134
Frommer, Harvey, 89, 180, 185-186

G
Gallagher, Joe, 227
Gallico, Paul, 125, 198
Garagiola, Joe, 122, 162
Garcia, Damaso, 241
Garcia, Rich, 137
Gardner, Billy, 238-239
Garvey, Steve, 136
Gazella, Mike, 220-222
Gehrig Lou "the Iron Horse," 12, 21, 24-25, 27, 32, 34, 42-43, 62, 71, 72, 73, 79, 123, 126, 147, 154, 158, 163, 165, 168, 173-174, 189, 198, 220-227, 246
Giambi, Jason, 42, 101
Giard, Joe, 221
Gibbons, John, 39
Gibbs, Jake, 239
Gionfriddo, Joe, 191
Girardi, Joe, 242-244
Girsch, George, 67
Glenn, Joe, 223-226
Gold Glove Award, 38, 160
Golenbock, Peter, 19
Gómez, Lefty, 12, 122, 159, 189-190, 216, 223-228, 246
Gonder, Jesse, 238
Gooden, Dwight, 242, 245
Gordon, Joe, 27, 226-229
Gorman, Tom, 234-235
Gossage, Rich "Goose," 119-120, 241
Grabowski, Johnny, 221-222
Graham, Frank, 17, 146
Greenberg, Hank, 96
Griffith Stadium, 106-108
Grim, Bob, 236-237
Grimes, Oscar, 229
Grimsley, Jason, 245
Guidry, Ron, 27, 87, 240-241
Gullett, Don, 240-241
Gumpert, Randy, 230

H

Hadley, Bump, 224-227
Hageman, William, 74
Haines, Hinkey, 220
Hale, Bob, 238
Hansen, Thor, 186
Hargrove, Mike, 152
Harris, Bucky, 230
Hayes, Charlie, 242
Healy, Fran, 240-241
Heath, Mike, 241
Heffner, Don, 224-225
Heilmann, Harry, 28
Heimach, Fred, 222
Hemingway, Ernest, 77
Hemsley, Rollie, 229
Henderson, Rickey, 113, 121
Hendrick, Harvey, 220
Hendricks, Ellie, 240
Henrich, Tommy, 12, 27, 34, 123, 128, 190, 200, 218, 225-228, 230-232
Hernández, Orlando "El Duque," 41, 48, 139, 217, 243-245
Herskowitz, Mickey, 79-80
Hildebrand, Oral, 227
Hill, Glenallen, 245
Hiller, Frank, 231
Hoag, Myril, 223-226
Hofmann, Fred, 220
Hogue, Bobby, 234
Holmes, Tommy, 65, 84
Holtzman, Ken, 240-241
Honig, Donald, 74, 107, 176
Hopp, Johnny, 232-234
Hornsby, Rogers, 185
Houdini, Harry, 210
Houk, Ralph, 36, 230-235, 238-239
Howard, Elston, 22, 46, 236-239
Howard, Matt, 242
Howley, Dan, 33
Howser, Dick, 241
Hoyt, Waite, 15, 147, 149, 163, 165, 180, 188, 203, 218, 220-222, 246
Huggins, Miller, 62, 74, 145, 149, 200, 206, 220-222, 246
Hunter, Billy, 236
Hunter, Jim "Catfish," 16, 21, 27, 121, 240-241, 246

I

Irabu, Hideki, 243-244

J

Jackson, Reggie, 9, 21, 27, 86, 91-92, 116, 121, 123, 129, 136, 145, 153, 155, 240-241, 246
James, Bill, 162
James, Dion, 242
James, Johnny, 237
Jensen, Jackie, 232-234
Jeter, Derek, 3, 6, 27, 49, 51, 94, 95, 102, 116-118, 137, 141, 144, 154, 161, 168, 195, 216, 242-245
Jimenez, Angelo, 244
John, Tommy, 208
Johnson, Billy, 229-233
Johnson, Cliff, 240-241
Johnson, Darrell, 237
Johnson, Deron, 238
Johnson, Don, 230, 232
Johnson, Ernie, 220
Johnson, Hank, 222-223
Johnson, Lance, 245
Johnson, Randy "Big Unit," 19, 140, 178
Johnson, Roy, 224-225
Johnstone, Jay, 241
Jones, Chipper, 102
Jones, Sam, 220
Jordan, Michael, 103
Jorgens, Art, 223-227
Jose, Felix, 245
Judge, Joe, 148
Justice, David, 245

K

Kahn, Roger, 87, 119, 150
Kaline, Al, 110
Kammeyer, Bob, 241
Kansas City Athletics, 11, 135
Kansas City Royals, 150
Keeler, Willie, 246
Keller, Charlie "King Kong," 27, 227-231, 234
Kelly, Pat, 242
Kelly, Roberto, 245
Kelly, Tom, 103
Kennedy, John F., 199
Kennedy, Adam, 144
Key, Jimmy, 242
Kieran, John, 71

Kingman, Dave, 113, 240
Klapisch, Bob, 102
Kleinhans, Ted, 224
Klutts, Mickey, 240-241
Knickerbocker, Bill, 226-227
Knoblauch, Chuck, 243-245
Koenig, Mark, 16, 22, 27, 74, 209, 221-222
Konrad, Kerry, 116-117
Konstanty, Jim, 236
Koufax, Sandy, 134
Kraly, Steve, 235
Kramer, Jack, 233
Kryhoski, Dick, 231
Kubek, Tony, 27, 36, 130, 149, 237-239
Kucks, Johnny, 12, 194, 236-237
Kuzava, Bob, 58, 233-235

L

Lally, Richard, 110
Landis, Judge Kenesaw Mountain, 47
Larsen, Don, 123, 129-130, 194, 236-237
Lary, Lyn, 223
Lasorda, Tommy, 160
Lavagetto, Cookie, 191
Lazzeri, Tony "Poosh'Em Up," 29, 159, 168, 190, 221-225, 246
Ledee, Ricky, 243-245
Leiter, Al, 154, 177
Lemon, Bob, 119, 241
Lenox Hill Hospital, 63
Leyritz, Jim, 242, 244-245
Lieb, Fred G., 169
Lincoln Center, 171
Lindblad, Paul, 241
Lindell, Johnny, 228-232
Linn, Ed, 179, 181
Linz, Phil, 177, 239
Locklear, Gene, 240
Lollar, Sherm, 230
Long, Dale, 239
Lopat, Ed "Eddie," 12, 84, 231-235
Lopez, Al, 84
Lopez, Hector, 238-239
Los Angeles (California) Angels, 42, 143-144, 212
Los Angeles Dodgers, 13, 136, 160

Louis, Joe, 146
Lowell, Mike, 243
Lucadello, Johnny, 230
Luciano, Ron, 184
Luke, Matt, 242
Lumpe, Jerry, 236-237
Lupica, Mike, 90
Lyle, Sparky, 27, 87, 160, 240-241
Lyons, Al, 230

M

Maas, Duke, 237
Macfayden, Danny, 223
Mack, Connie, 11, 74, 149, 167
MacPhail, Larry, 246
MacPhail, Lee, 246
Madison, Dave, 232
Maglie, Sal, 237
Makosky, Frank, 225
Malone, Pat, 224-225
Mantle, Mickey "the Commerce Comet," 9, 12, 22-23, 25, 36, 38, 42, 44, 54, 79-80, 105-114, *109*, 110-114, 116, 123, 131, 134-135, 154, 157, 163-164, 166, 169, 178, 192-194, 201, 209, 211, 213, 217, 233-239, 246
Manto, Jeff, 244
Mapes, Cliff, 231-233
Maris, Pat, 199
Maris, Roger, 27, 46, 85-86, 123, 131-134, 198-199, 215, 238-239
Marshall, Cuddles, 231
Martin, Billy, 12, 36, 45, 59, 75, 113, 128, 192-193, 232-236, 240-241
Martinez, Pedro, 180
Martinez, Tino, 27, 37, 242-245
Marx Brothers, 146
Mathewson, Christy, 134
Matsui, Hideki, 39, 140, 208
Mattingly, Don, 27, 37, 93, 96
May, Carlos, 240
Mays, Carl, 188, 220
Mays, Willie, 113-114, 163, 192
Mazeroski, Bill, 130

McCall, Larry, 240-241
McCarthy, Joe, 32, 77, 149, 223-229, 246
McCarver, Tim, 183
McDermott, Mickey, 236
McDevitt, Danny, 238
McDonald, Jim, 234-235
McDougald, Gil, 233-237
McGraw, John, 45, 59, 149, 188-189
McIntosh, Tim, 242
McNally, Mike, 220
McQuinn, George, 230
Meier, Jeffrey, 137
Mendoza, Ramiro, 242-243
Merriwell, Frank, 33
Messersmith, Andy, 241
Metheny, Bud, 229
Meusel, Bob, 12, *30*, 31, 147, 163, 168, 220-222
Miller, Bill, 234-235
Miller, Rick, 87
Milwaukee Brewers, 96
Minnesota Twins, 103, 138, 208
Miranda, Willy, 235
Mitchell, Bo, 130
Mitchell, Dale, 130
Mize, Johnny, 231-235
Mole, Fenton, 231
Monroe, Marilyn, 120
Monroe, Zach, 237
Moore, Wilcy, 33, 221-223
Morehart, Ray, 221
Morgan, Tom, 233-234, 236
Mosedale, John, 14, 29, 31-32, 43, 66, 68, 124, 126, 146, 148, 163, 171
Munson, Thurman, 27, 86, 90, 240-241
Murcer, Bobby, 27, 36, 38
Murderers Row, 145, 151
Murphy, Johnny, 223-229
Musial, Stan, 78, 96
Mussina, Mike, 144

N

National Baseball Hall of Fame, 28, 34, 57, 68, 79, 83, 91, 96, 110, 158-159, 162-167, 215, 246
National League, 23, 65, 134, 187, 190, 192, 196
Neel, Eric, 99
Nelson, Jeff, 242-243, 245

Nettles, Graig, 27, 36, *88*, 89, 122, 160, 168, 205, 213, 240-241
Nevel, Ernie, 232-233
New York Daily Mirror, 67
New York Daily News, 90, 125
New York Giants, 22, 45, 149, 171, 176, 187-190, 192, 195
New York Herald Tribune, 71
New York Mets, 39, 83, 94, 120, 141, 154, 183, 187, 195-196
New York Post, 34, 39
New York Press, 171
New York Sun, 18, 174
New York Times, 15, 29, 71, 125, 127, 131
Newsday, 90
Newsom, Bobo, 230
Newsweek, 25
Niarhos, Gus, 231
Noren, Irv, 234-236

O

O'Neill, Paul, 26-27, 37, 44, 48, 93, 161, 242-245
Oakland A's, 11, 13, 151
Oklahoma, University of, 213
Ortiz, David, 96, 181
Ostrowski, Joe, 232-234
Overmire, Stubby, 233
Owen, Mickey, 123, 128, 190

P

Pafko, Andy, 23
Page, Joe, 120, 191, 230-232
Palmer, Jim, 87
Paschal, Ben, 221-222
Patterson, Gil, 240
Patterson, Red, 108
Pearson, Monte, 224-227
Peek, Steve, 228
Pennock, Herb, 28, 147, 180, 220-223, 246
Pepitone, Joe, 27, 239
Perez, Marty, 240
Pettitte, Andy, 39, 104, 242-245
Philadelphia Athletics, 11-12, 71, 96, 123, 126, 135, 158, 167

Philadelphia Phillies, 126
Phillips, Eddie, 223
Phillips, Jack, 230-231
Piazza, Mike, 120, 195
Pillette, Duane, 231
Piniella, Lou, 96, 119, 240-241
Pipgras, George, 147, 220-223
Pipp, Wally, 126, 220
Pittsburgh Pirates, 55, 96, 126
Podres, Johnny, 193
Polo Grounds, 171, 188
Polonia, Luis, 245
Porterfield, Bob, 231-232
Posada, Jorge, 38, 50, 99, 118, 143, 242-245
Powell, Jake, 189, 224-227
Price, Jim, 171
Pride of the Yankees, 21
Priddy, Jerry, 228

Q
Queen, Mel, 230
Quinn, Bob, 163

R
Raines, Tim, 151, 242-243
Ramos, Pedro, 106
Randolph, Willie, 240-241
Raschi, Vic, 12, 27, 35, 230-235
Reed, Jack, 238-239
Reniff, Hal, 238
Renna, Bill, 235
Reston, James, 131
Reynolds, Allie "the Chief," 12, 27, 35, 191-193, 200, 215, 230-235
Rhodes, Gordon, 223
Richardson, Bobby, 27, 236-239
Rickey, Branch, 80
Rivera, Mariano, 9, 27, 41-42, 49, 98-99, 100, 101-103, 143, 242
Rivera, Ruben, 242
Rivers, Mickey, 38, 121, 240-241
Rizzuto, Phil, 12, 35, 78, 81, 178, 228, 230-236, 246
Robertson, Gene, 222
Robinson, Aaron, 229-230
Robinson, Brooks, 36

Robinson, Eddie, 236
Robinson, Frank, 96
Robinson, Jackie, 128, 191-193
Robinson, "Uncle" Wilbert, 55
Rodriguez, Alex "A-Rod," 40-41, 96, 97, 103, 117, 140, 142, 156, 182, 210
Roettger, Oscar, 220
Roffetti, Tony, 29
Rogers, Kenny, 242
Rolfe, Red, 189, 224-228
Roosevelt, Franklin D., 146
Root, Charlie, 127
Rosar, Buddy, 227-228
Ross, Robert Alexander, 5
Rovell, Darren, 116
Royal, Darrell, 213
Rudi, Joe, 204
Ruether, Dutch, 221
Ruffing, Red, 180, 190, 223-228, 246
Ruppert, Jacob, 19, 176
Russo, Marius, 227-229
Ruth, George Herman "Babe," "the Bambino," 12, 25, 27, 31, 34, 42, 47, 62, 66-68, 69, 70-71, 73, 75, 79, 105, 107, 114, 124-125, 127, 131, 133-134, 146-147, 151, 154, 158-159, 163, 165, 168-169, 173-174, 179-180, 188-189, 197, 202, 206, 215, 217, 220-223, 246
Ryan, Nolan, 87
Ryan, Rosy, 222

S
Sain, Johnny, 233-235
Saltzgaver, Jack, 223-225
San Francisco Giants, 96
Sanford, Fred, 231-233
Saraceno, Jon, 154
Saturday Night Live, 22
Scarborough, Ray, 234-235
Schaeffer, Harry, 234
Schalk, Roy, 223
Schallock, Art, 233, 235
Schang, Wally, 180, 220
Schmitz, Johnny, 234
Schult, Art, 235
Scott, Everett, 180, 220
Scully, Vin, 173

Sears, Ken, 229
Seattle Mariners, 52
Seaver, Tom, 87
Seeds, Bob, 224
Segrist, Kal, 234
Selkirk, George, 224-228
Sepkowski, Ted, 230
Sewell, Joe, 124, 223
Shantz, Bobby, 237
Shawkey, Bob, 220-221
Shea, Spec, 230-231, 233
Shealy, Al, 222
Sheed, Wilfrid, 169, 171
Sheehy, Pete, 75
Sheffield, Gary, 41, 50, 140, 144, 156
Sheldon, Rollie, 238-239
Sheppard, Bob, 129, 157, 218
Sherman, Joel, 39
Sherrill, Dennis, 241
Siebern, Norm, 236-237
Sierra, Ruben, 242
Silvera, Charlie, 231-236
Silvestri, Ken, 228, 230
Simmons, Al, 158
Simpson, Harry, 237
Skizas, Lou, 236
Skowron, Bill "Moose," 12, 194, 212, 236-239
Slaughter, Enos, 236-237
Small, Aaron, 40, 208
Smith, Elmer, 220
Smith, Ken, 57
Sojo, Luis, 27, 139, 242-245
Soriano, Alfonso, 141, 244-245
Spahn, Warren, 83
Speaker, Tris, 66, 163, 215
Spencer, Jim, 241
Spencer, Shane, 243-245
Sporting News, 166
Sports Illustrated, 196
St. Louis Browns, 33, 206
St. Louis Cardinals, 80, 96, 104, 195
Stafford, Bill, 238-239
Stainback, Tuck, 229
Staley, Gerry, 236
Stallard, Tracy, 132
Stanceu, Charley, 228
Stanley, Fred, 240-241
Stanton, Mike, 243-245
Starr, Dick, 230

Steinbrenner, George, 18, 26, 37, 48, 117, 120, 152, 155-156, 161, 212-214, 216

Stengel, Charles Dillon "Casey," "the Old Perfessor," 9, 22, 31, 36, 44-47, 53, 57, 59, 61-64, 74-75, 78, 83-85, 108, 110-112, 116, 120, 128, 130, 164, 167-168, 189, 206-207, 217, 231-237, 246

Stengel, Edna, 207

Stine, Lee, 226

Stirnweiss, Snuffy, 229-232

Stobbs, Chuck, 106, 108

Stottlemyre, Mel, 47, 138

Stout, Glenn, 20, 156

Strawberry, Darryl, 47, 104, 242-244

Sturdivant, Tom, 111, 236-237

Sturm, Johnny, 228

Subway Series, 7, 187, 189-193, 195-196

Sullivan, Haywood, 182

Sundra, Steve, 224, 226-227

Sveum, Dale, 243

T

Tarasco, Tony, 137, 244

Terry, Ralph, 166, 236, 238-239

Texas, University of, 213

Thomas, Lee, 238

Thomas, Myles, 221-222

Thomas, Stan, 240

Thomasson, Gary, 241

Thompson, Ryan, 245

Thomson, Bobby, 192

Throneberry, Marv, 237

Tiant, Luis, 122

Tidrow, Dick, 240-241

Torgeson, Earl, 238

Toronto Blue Jays, 39, 42, 98, 141, 208

Torre, Joe, 17, 37, 39-41, 46, 48, 94, 101, 104, 141, 151-153, 161, 173, 184, 210, 212, 214, 216, 242-245

Torrez, Mike, 136, 240

Towers, Josh, 42

Trammell, Bubba, 39

Tresh, Tom, 238-239

Triandos, Gus, 235

Trucks, Virgil, 237

Tudisco, Circo, 186

Tullius, John, 149

Turley, Bob, 236-239

Turner, Chris, 245

Turner, Jim, 229

V

Valentine, Bobby, 94, 101, 151

Vance, Joe, 225-226

Verducci, Tom, 196

Vizcaino, Jose, 245

W

Wagner, Honus, 78

Waite, Bill, 176

Wakefield, Dick, 232

Walker, Dixie, 224

Wang, Chien-Ming, 39

Ward, Aaron, 220

Washburn, George, 228

Washington Senators, 106-108, 148

Weatherly, Roy, 229

Weaver, Earl, 91

Weiss, George, 207, 246

Weiss, Hazel, 207

Wells, David, 123, 129, 138, 202, 243

Wells, Ed, 223

Wensloff, Butch, 229-230

Wera, Julie, 221

Wetteland, John, 242

Wheeler, Lonnie, 108, 114, 135

White, Jo-Jo, 46

White, Roy, 240-241

Wicker, Kemp, 224-225

Wickman, Bob, 242

Wiesler, Bob, 233

Wight, Bill, 230

Wilbert, Warren, 74

Wilkinson, Bud, 213

Williams, Bernie, 14, 27, 38, 51-52, 98, 122, 137, 140, 196, 208, 242-245

Williams, Gerald, 242

Williams, Ted, 47, 111, 176, 185-186

Wilson, Archie, 233-234

Wilson, George, 236

Wilson, Hack, 185

Winfield, Dave, 115

Witek, Mickey, 231

Witt, Whitey, 220

Wojciechowski, Gene, 118, 141, 184

Wolfe, Thomas, 158

Woodling, Gene, 112, 231-235

Workman, Hank, 232

World Series, 26, 38-39, 54, 59, 68, 94, 96, 104, 107, 120, 126-130, 136, 145, 153-154, 160-161, 166, 182, 187, 189-194, 196, 200, 212

Wynn, Early, 44

Wynn, Jim, 240

Y

Yankee Stadium, 11, 16, 19, 23, 25, 56, 62, 77, 106-107, *112*, 117, 135, 138, 157, 169, 172-176, 178

You Can't Go Home Again, 158

Yount, Robin, 96

Z

Zachary, Tom, 222

Zeber, George, 240-241

Zimmer, Don, 104, 122

Zuber, Bill, 229

Printed in the USA
CPSIA information can be obtained
at www.ICGtesting.com
JSHW082157140824
68134JS00014B/287

9 781581 825268